# BEHIND *the* POWER

## Raw Courage to Triumph Over Challenges and Connect with What's Possible

ALLYSON ROBERTS

ISBN: 978-1-7375511-0-2 (paperback)
ISBN: 978-1-7375511-1-9 (ebook)

Library of Congress Control Number: 2021914061

Printed in Woodstock, Georgia, USA by Allyson Roberts.



For more information, visit AllysonRoberts.com.

# TABLE OF CONTENTS

# DEDICATION

This book is dedicated to the women who stepped up, spoke up, and showed up to become the best versions of themselves (so far). They should be applauded for coming out of hiding to face their absolute deepest pain so they could embrace their power.

It's also dedicated to you, for reading the book and taking the steps to finally, once and for all, love yourself, be yourself, and give yourself the life you deserve.

Welcome to ***Behind the Power,*** which is everything inside of you.

# INTRODUCTION

*Look within and allow more light into the sacred experience we call life.*

This book is a glimpse into the mighty power that lies within thirteen amazing women. While we know that power exists in millions of other women, too, many of us are afraid to claim it. We tamp ourselves down out of fear of being found out. We believe that our most painful story is the death of us, not the birth of some of our greatest accomplishments. We hide behind what's real. We are so afraid that if people really knew us, they'd immediately reject us. That our lives would somehow be ruined. The truth is, our greatest power lies beneath our greatest pain.

Five years ago, I was sitting in a conference in Vancouver, and I was overwhelmed by the outpouring of courage shared by everyone there. I never dreamed I could get on a stage and reveal my personal pain with three hundred and fifty other women hanging onto my every word. It changed my life. Actually, it changed everything.

This book was borne from that experience, and I knew the timing had to be exactly right. If it were too soon, something wouldn't feel right with the project, and too late — precious stories from my clients would be lost. When COVID hit the world — our world — I knew that the time to help other women connect to the souls of the fabric of our goddess energy was NOW!

Each of the women in this book has a completely different journey, but something they all share is the willingness to look within. They each understand that the one thing that must remain steadfast, long after the experience has come and gone, is self-love. This only comes from self-awareness. As you read their stories, you will see that none of them is perfect. Not a single one of them believes they have all the answers. Each of these warriors carries within her a profound wisdom of knowing that authenticity is not about getting it all right, but rather, it's about admitting when we are completely wrong in our thought process.

Selecting these women was more than an intellectual process; it was also an inspiring and spiritual journey. I didn't place names in a hat, or randomly invite hundreds of women to follow alongside me on this year-long adventure. Instead, I hand-selected each one, guided solely by Spirit and my intuition. I knew that they would have to truly be ready to up-level, ready to admit their truth, not only to themselves but to you, and ready to share their souls in a heartfelt way so that your path is illuminated.

*Behind the Power* is a message from Spirit through each of these willing souls set with the intention to help you grow, align, reconnect with your deepest purpose and passion, and shine! We didn't mess around in our preparation. We didn't hold back. Oh, believe me, some wanted to play really small and write about issues that didn't dig deep enough into their pain to truly help you heal. But, as you will learn on this journey, our reptilian brain seduces us to take a small seat, hide and wither until the time comes that we simply can't do it any longer.

These amazing storytellers know how important your growth is, not only for your own journey, but for all the lives you touch on a regular basis. They understand that sometimes the first step to our greatest healing is knowing that we are not alone. In that awareness, we can finally give ourselves permission to listen to our intuition, face our mental conflict, and choose to make our lives whole again.

My hope is that you will allow yourself to be touched by these incredible women; that you see yourself in each of them; and that your heart is broken wide open to allow more light into the sacred experience we call life.

# A SPECIAL GIFT FROM ALLYSON

From this amazing book, you'll understand that you are not alone, no matter what you are facing right now. Through the moving stories inside these pages, you'll discover that there is hope, and that it's possible to accomplish the goals to make your dreams come true.

But let's face it, life can be challenging. This is especially true when you don't understand what's happening inside (or outside) of you. You do all the right things. You are "a good person." You're responsible, caring, loving, compassionate, generous, kind . . . and yet you somehow always end up right back where you started – no matter what you try to change in your life to create a different reality.

It's not you . . . it's your brain. It's the truth.

Your brain has a part of it called "the reptilian" and its job is to keep you safe, to keep you the same. Yet to make changes in your life and get different results than what you've had so far, you have to do things differently.

That doesn't mean go out and try many different things (or the same thing) over and over because that only yields more frustration, and you won't be any further ahead. In fact, you'll likely move backwards.

To help you begin creating the right foundation for making the changes you want to make, I have prepared a special gift just for you: *Becoming the Boss of Your Brain!* This gift will help you slow down, acknowledge your feelings and emotions, and honor who you are. You've made it through all of life's challenges you've faced so far, and you **can** create a different life than the one you have right now.

Just go to AllysonRoberts.com/gift and tell us where to send it.

Grateful to be part of your journey!

**Allyson**

# CHAPTER 1

# UNFORGOTTEN LOVE BY CINDY TURNER

*When Alzheimer's tests "in sickness and health," a wife turned caregiver learns the importance of putting herself first. Learning to believe and trust in her abilities and connection with the divine opened doors that were once invisible.*

The phone rings and I jump to answer it.

It is Jim. Thank God! I had been waiting to hear from him. Why is he so late? What could be wrong?

"I'm lost," he says.

"What do you mean you're lost? Where are you?" My heart is pounding, I'm feeling afraid, and even worse, angry that he is lost. Fear always makes me angry.

"I'm not sure. I left work and started for home, but I must have made a wrong turn. I have no idea where I am," said Jim.

My mind is spinning. Oh, dear Lord, the doctor said he would get to this stage and if he got lost, even just once, he would have to quit driving. How am I going to be able to get him home? This cannot be happening. This *cannot* be happening! My brain starts throwing ideas at me. Do I try to drive to him and have him follow me home? Do I have a car service pick him up? Do I call the police? Do I try to help him find his way home? What can I do?

He is short tempered as well. Naturally, he is upset that he is lost, embarrassed that he has to ask me for help, and afraid he will not be able to find his way home. Short tempers and fear do not make for easy communicating.

I pull up his location on the GPS on my phone app (grateful that my granddaughter had shown me this app and installed it for me just a few months earlier) to see where he is and start telling him how to get home. I force myself to stay calm and make a concerted effort to keep my voice soft and confident, while on the inside I am falling apart. Little by little, street by street, I start telling him where to turn and where to go straight. It is tedious work, and his phone only has so much power left, and of course, he doesn't have a charger with him. I didn't know what we would do if his battery died. This is so much stress. I feel queasy and afraid. My head is pounding with pure fear.

He would miss a turn and I would have to try to explain to him how to turn around or make a U-turn, or go blocks out of his way to get back on track. Apparently, the terms "right" and "left" were no longer in his memory banks and it was exceedingly difficult to make him understand which way to go. Never mind trying to use north, south, east, or west. To make matters worse, he was unable to read the street signs for some reason. I don't know if it was because he couldn't locate them, or he couldn't read. It was dark out and everything seemed like life and death to me. For nearly two hours I gave him directions and walked him through his mistakes and his successes.

Finally, he was in our neighborhood, recognized his surroundings, and we hung up. I let myself break down and bawl. It was so disheartening and frightening. I was sick with worry and fear. I didn't want him to see me in this state, so I pulled myself together and watched out the window for his car.

As he entered the house, I noticed his anxiety and fear mixed with the relief of being home. He was scared and his was the saddest face I had ever seen. This precious man was my hero, my Prince Charming. He always took care of me and stood as my knight in shining armor, complete with a white horse. And now, he was diagnosed with dementia and starting to have serious memory problems.

I simply refused to believe the diagnosis, sure that this would be a temporary situation. Our story did not include dementia. We were living the happily ever after story. No, it was not going to end this way. But this episode was strong evidence that he was most definitely losing his memory. His MRIs showed that he had experienced several strokes in his life, but he had no memory of any times that he felt anything that would indicate this. So, I hung on to the hope that this was a vascular issue and could get better.

As I sat looking at this man that meant the world to me, I thought back to the person I was before him: a single mom, divorced, and coming from a really bad marriage. I had no self-esteem or confidence. The first husband had taken a chunk of my soul. I was never planning on another marriage. I lived with depression and anxiety. I took antidepressants, but they never really fixed the problem. There was something wrong at a deep level. I even tried a psychiatrist, but that was all pills and no help.

But Jim, Jim was a surprise, a dose of medicine. He was kind and loving and giving. He was upbeat and positive and never judged me. He put the pieces back together and helped me see that I was OK. He loved my daughter as if she were his own without playing "dad" to her. And when the grandkids came along, no one was a more excited and engaged grandfather. I would never meet another Jim. I was just sure of it. He was special.

We had spent the last half a dozen years traveling all over the world and having the times of our lives: London, Rome, Paris, Dublin, Edinburgh, Athens, and planned to keep going. I would wake up in a hotel in Paris and there was Jim, holding a cup of coffee for me and telling me what a beautiful day it was outside and how beautiful I was. Truly magical times. A day did not go by without lots of I love yous and You are beautifuls.

I thought about how special he was with my daughter, whom he loved deeply and wished was his own. He was amazing with the grandchildren and especially loving to my mother. He would go by himself to visit Mom and take her pizza and watch ballgames with her almost every Sunday. I don't care who you are, that is not a common thing for a son-in-law.

I snapped out of the past when I heard a drawer slam and looked around to see Jim fuming because he wasn't able to find his phone charger. Jim was not one to lose his patience or temper about such minor things, but he was rattled and scared. I helped him find it. He then went off to take a shower.

As time passed, Jim misplaced everything. I would spend hours looking for something that he wanted to find, only to find it in the trash or the refrigerator or never find it at all. His glasses, combs, remote controls, even clothes. One day he took off his glasses and just bent them to pieces right in front of me.

I needed magic and I was going to find it. I searched and allowed my mind to be open to all kinds of different possibilities that might make a difference in this diagnosis. I would not accept that he truly had dementia (especially Alzheimer's) because I was told there was no cure. How could there be no cure in this day and age?

I researched everything and tried everything that even hinted at being a deterrent to dementia or Alzheimer's. I have never been a good cook; I had no natural instinct for it. I don't know, something just happened when I applied heat. I cooked special recipes with spices from a far-off land where it was claimed that no one ever got Alzheimer's. Nevertheless, cook I did. I gave him herbs and vitamins and sought out healing techniques. My desperation was out of control and I would do anything to make this nightmare stop.

He became uninterested in food, wouldn't eat his meals, and would barely drink water. Even his favorite foods were not a temptation for him any longer. He stopped wearing some of his clothes and only wanted certain shirts. He could no longer help with all the little chores around the house. When once he would have done all the grocery shopping and a lot of the cooking, the yard work, and the little maintenance tasks, now he sat and did nothing. Needless to say, all these tasks fell on me to handle and added to my stress level.

One of the most difficult things for me to accept and handle was when Jim lost control of his bladder and bowels. I knew this would have been the height of indignity for him and he would hate this so much if he were able to actually understand the situation. His body simply wasn't sending or receiving the right messages anymore. It was all normal according to the doctor. So our world started including diapers and bed pads. My laundry duties tripled.

It was difficult to tell if Jim could understand the severity of the situation. He ate only chips and ice cream. He tried to do everything I asked him to do and for the most part, maintained a positive outlook. He even continued telling me I was pretty, which I loved. I considered it a good sign that he still knew me, until I heard him telling other people the same thing. It was frightening to think that we were not going to have a future together. It was heartbreaking to see him lose touch with the grandkids.

I soothed myself with learning and research. While searching the internet, I found an online school for animal communication. Of course, animal communication wouldn't heal Jim, but it included classes about energy healing, along with communication, and I thought that this might be the miracle I needed. It would also give me something else to focus on. I had already completed all my training to be a Reiki Master. So I used Reiki on Jim daily, and though he wasn't improving, he was relaxed and calm, which I considered a win.

I wasn't sure it was possible to truly communicate with animals, but I knew that if there was anything I wanted to do, it was talk with my pets and all animals. Yes, it sounded too good to be true and I had been burned by believing in dreams before. I sincerely thought it would be one of those things that everyone else could do but I would not be able to.

Boy, was I wrong. I was surprised to discover I was able to communicate with so many species! Imagine how you would feel if you were truly able to get messages from the animals. It was magical. I talked with dogs, cats, horses, rabbits, pigs, goats, a fox, an orangutan, a gibbon, a chicken, and it was all fascinating. It completely changed how I thought about animals and their personal lives.

I worked hard and learned all the energy healing modalities and other techniques that might help Jim reclaim his memory. During this education, I graduated from school and became a professional animal communicator and energy healer.

All along, I was practicing everything I learned on Jim. Watching for miracles and determined that each new modality would be the silver bullet.

We became housebound, partly because of the pandemic with the COVID-19 virus, and partly because it became harder and harder to take Jim anywhere. I quit shopping for groceries and started having them delivered, same with the pet supplies. Jim would get distracted and wander off in stores, so I had to keep my eyes on him every second. Worse, he would often throw a loud tantrum if he didn't have something he wanted or if he thought someone did something to him. It was too difficult to manage him and shop at the same time. When one of his doctor's appointments had to be done via telephone rather than in person, the doctor asked me a series of questions, then determined that Jim was qualified for hospice.

Hospice! Does that word really mean he is near the end? Were we already to the stage of hospice? All my learning and attempts at healing were worthless. He was dying and there was nothing I could do about it. I had failed. This was a serious blow to me. I still believed I could save him, but the doctor had just put him in hospice care. Of course, I would keep him at home and have them come here; I would not send him away unless it became absolutely necessary.

Nurses were in and out. Aides were in and out. Jim became more and more withdrawn and unhappy. Hallucinations were occurring that frightened me. Medications were changed around. Constant care was needed. He kept telling me that people were hitting him in the head with rocks. Thankfully, I mentioned this to one of the nurses and was told that she thought he was having headaches and didn't know how to tell me that. I started giving him ibuprofen and the rocks went away.

It became important that I monitor all the television viewing because he could not distinguish between the show and reality. After he had told me that he had been shot a few times, I realized he was getting that from the television. Before his illness, he loved cop shows, but they had a lot of shooting and violence. So, music became the main form of entertainment for him. He still loved music, and it was relatively safe for him to listen to.

I had to purchase a baby monitor so I could keep an eye on him when I was working in my study on class work or paying bills. I had to get an alarm for the bed so I would hear him if he got up at night. This became necessary after he did get up one night, opened the back door, and set off the house alarm. Was he really going to go outside? Would he wander off and get lost?

The thought of him being lost at this stage scared the life out of me. Plus, all the pets, especially the cats who are "indoor cats," were trying to go with him. I stopped sleeping. The fear of what would happen if I wasn't awake was overwhelming. The bed alarm at least allowed me to sleep a few hours every night.

In all the time I was researching and learning how to save my husband, I learned how to do animal communication, Emotional Freedom Technique, Scalar Wave, acupressure, medical intuition, sound therapy, and of course, I became a Reiki Master. I learned how to do subjective conversations and The Silva Method. I learned about crystals and essential oils and herbs and ayurvedic medicine. I learned about the five elements and the Akashic Records. I literally tried everything I could get my hands on.

Most of all, I learned about myself. In all this panic to heal Jim, I was healing myself and preparing for the future in a completely different way than ever before. I learned to believe and trust in my abilities and connection with the divine. I became stronger and more confident. I learned how to do everything that needed to be done. I learned to take care of myself even while caring for him. I learned how to love myself.

It was a journey and still is. Being aware of how I am thinking and feeling so I can adjust to maintain a positive and productive lifestyle takes a lot of work. It is the sacred work of joy. It makes all the difference in your day-to-day living. Mindset is absolutely everything. I received excellent coaching and tools that changed my life. I became a woman who could do anything. I became a woman who has courage, strength, power, grace and most of all, wisdom. I became me, my authentic self.

## NOTES AND REFLECTIONS

## PATH TO YOUR POWER

### MAKE YOURSELF A HIGH PRIORITY

When I was my beloved Jim's caregiver, I'd forgotten how to take care of me. Everything was about him because I loved him so, so much. During the last stages of his life, I was reminded how important it is to put me first. I also want you to make yourself a HIGH priority. This is my daily routine. I hope you find some courage here.

Commit to a Daily Meditation even if it's only for five minutes. You'd be surprised how easy it is to carve out five minutes once you decide to do it. The thing that helped me the most is getting quiet and very still. The type of quiet where you are listening to your soul. Guided meditations are wonderful under the right set of circumstances, but it is important that we all spend time in quiet meditation with ourselves and/or Source every day.

Please care for your body. You are that important. While it may sound simple, when we are overwhelmed, things like bathing, pampering, dressing, putting on make-up and doing our hair can take last priority – and they shouldn't. When you care for your physical body, you just feel better all over and it promotes a more positive outlook. Try taking care of the outside and see what happens on the inside.

Eliminate negative self-talk. You are your biggest critic. Stop beating up on yourself and give yourself some encouragement. If no one else is being your cheerleader, then it is up to you! I find that even when people are being super sweet to me, sometimes it just doesn't matter. My self-talk can be nasty. It's then that I know it's time to take charge and change my language toward myself.

Work on your mindset every day. What are your priorities? Make sure you know them. Don't allow yourself to go on autopilot. Pay attention to what you believe and know why you believe it. Make sure your actions match your core values.

Ask for help; it won't happen by itself. If you need support, you have to ask for it. You can ask friends, professionals, or my personal favorite, your soul and Source. Then, do what feels right. Don't ask for help and then refuse to receive it. You're worth more than that!

## ABOUT

Cindy Turner is a Spiritual Sage with a toolbox that includes many skills and resources such as Cognizant intuitive, communicator with nature, reiki healer, sound worker, and more. Her experience, combined with her wisdom guides, allows her to guide her clients through even the most difficult situations. She provides sound next steps and a "behind-the-scenes" view of what's happening in any given situation. Cindy's clients come away from her sessions with renewed hope and an action plan. You can find out more information and how to book your next session with Cindy at https://TheSoulForest.com.

Taking a glimpse into Cindy's personal life, she grew up in Ohio but has lived in Texas most of her life and has the Texan drawl to prove it. She worked in the corporate world in human resources until retirement, when she stepped into her new purpose and passion. Cindy has a daughter and three grandchildren, two dogs, and two cats. She adores animals (and people) all over the world.

# NOTES AND REFLECTIONS

# CHAPTER 2

# PAYTON ROSE BY KAREN THOMAS

*A promise to a dying dog transforms a lifelong struggle with disassociating, putting personal needs last, and eating disorders into a passion pursuit. Founder of non-profit sanctuary for dogs reaching end-of-life transitions shares her journey.*

My heart is racing, the sweat is dripping down my forehead, and my throat is burning as I'm hunched over the toilet bowl, frantically trying to get rid of the food I just ate. After several minutes of vomiting, I feel a momentary rush of deep relief where I can breathe again. I stand up to wash my sweat- and tear-stained face and rinse my mouth, and suddenly, I'm back in my body staring into my empty eyes, barely recognizing who this person is in the mirror. How did I get here yet again? Shame and guilt rush over me, each time getting heavier and heavier as the feeling of relief that purging brings gets less and less. Bulimia is controlling my life.

I was born into a world of chaos, the youngest of five children. My mother suffered from extreme anxiety and was hospitalized shortly after I was born. Due to her mental illness, she was incapable of bonding with me and was never there for me emotionally as I grew up. My father was a charming but controlling man who worked a lot.

My brothers made many bad choices, adding to the toxic home environment and abuse. While being sexually molested at age four and a half, I learned to disassociate from my body; I would stare at the wall until I saw an angel appear. After that, I felt like I was flying and time-traveling through space until it seemed safe to come back to my body.

At the age of seven, I begged my mother to take me to a local animal rescue to volunteer. When I picked up the first puppy, we locked eyes and instantly recognized each other's pain. We had a telepathic conversation that lasted a few seconds but conveyed a great amount of information. We both shared with each other that we had been abandoned in many ways, and that together, we could heal. This puppy and I were experiencing similar heartache in different bodies. From that moment, I knew in my soul that I could breathe again. I found my purpose for living.

I immediately set out to learn everything about dogs, burying my head in library books about breeds, temperament, grooming, and much more. I was searching for why I felt so much more connected to them than to humans.

When I was eight, my oldest brother, Tony, acquired a black poodle, Jazz, and I quickly fell in love. I finally felt like there was someone in the house I could relate to. A year later, my parents agreed to get me a dog, a young female terrier, who I named Daisy. Daisy was my heart and soul, my very best friend. I finally had friends, Jazz and Daisy, who understood me.

The deep shame and guilt I carried from childhood gave birth to perfectionism. I learned to restrict my calories and exercise obsessively to control my weight. I was a straight A student and studied nursing in college because taking care of people was natural to me.

Early in my career I began attracting charming partners that were simply holograms of my father. I eventually married a man who I met at the hospital, "Collin," who was completing his medical residency. He was covertly narcissistic but wasn't physically abusive, so he looked like a gem. On my wedding day, I knew in my heart that I was making a mistake. Once again, I found myself disassociating from my body to avoid the emotional and mental pain. But I didn't dare call it off for fear of disappointing both our families and friends, all who came to the ceremony.

After three years of numbing myself through this toxic marriage by binging on food and overexercising, we decided to go our separate ways. I moved to south Florida, where my sister lived. At this point, I didn't know anything about myself: who I was, my likes, my passions, my hopes and dreams . . . nothing. I felt emotionally dead. All I knew was that I wanted peace.

Within a week of moving to Florida, I got a job at the local hospital. But starting a new stressful job, working twelve-hour shifts while filing for divorce, gave me little time to decompress and heal. About three weeks into my new routine, I walked into work one morning and saw a photo of a dog taped to a piece of paper hanging at the nurses' station. The note under the photo read: "free to a good home, male."

I stared at this dog's picture for a full five minutes. All of the feelings about dogs that I used to have as a child started to trickle through my heart. I felt safety, joy, love, and peace for the first time in years. I knew I needed to adopt him. I called the owner that evening and she said he was a "bad dog." But I knew that there were no bad dogs; dogs are innately loving beings that sometimes make bad choices.

The next morning, I pulled up to her apartment and could hear loud, frightened barking. When she opened the door, I saw him barking, jumping, and lunging against his tether at me. He looked fearful, but also like he wanted to leave with me. She loaded the back of my truck with whatever dog food she had left and a few old, ragged toys. She untethered him and like a cannon ball, he shot down the steps and right into the back of my truck. He looked straight in my eyes and said, "I've been waiting for you, now let's go home!"

I named my handsome, energetic boy Bo, and we became instant best friends. He had numerous behavioral issues, but he was absolutely perfect for me, and we vowed to help each other heal. My spiritual journey started here, and I devoured books on spirituality, angels, and personal development. We also worked hard with a dog trainer.

Shortly after adopting Bo, I started volunteering at our local animal shelter, which ignited my soul. My spirit started to come alive. Homeless dogs became my passion. Each dog had a story to tell, as many suffered neglect and trauma. I knew in my heart they craved acceptance, safety, and love to start their healing process.

Over the next five years, I focused on expanding my spiritual growth through learning Reiki and Healing Touch. When Bo was eight years old, I adopted a second dog, Libby, a rambunctious puppy I met at the shelter. Despite my evolving spirit and the love of my incredible dogs, I still took care of everyone else first and put my own needs last.

In 2008, my oldest brother, Tony, died after a drug overdose. My parents took his death *hard*. My father's failing health quickly took a nose-dive. When my family turned to me, the nurse, to oversee his care, I returned to Pennsylvania. While he was still coherent enough to talk, he asked me to take care of my mother. Of course, I said I would. I did not know how to say no and had zero boundaries. I dutifully cared for my father until his death ten months later; I was his hospice nurse the last twenty-four hours of his life.

I brought my mother back to my parents' second home in Florida. I decided to move in with her temporarily to help. Months went by, and she seemed to be emotionally arrested, stuck deeply in grief, and not processing effectively. I was filled with anger: angry at my father for leaving me to deal with this, angry at myself for saying yes to picking up the pieces, and angry at my mother for, once again, not being there for me.

Being solely focused on herself and her own needs, my mother never recognized that managing all this was continuing to take a huge toll on my already fragile mental health. I had never had time and space to work through my emotions. Outwardly I seemed to be holding everything together. But deep inside was a tremendous amount of anger and resentment, bubbling like a volcano ready to erupt. One evening after a long, stressful day at work, I started numbing myself with food again.

Feeling completely defeated, I told myself that I really had no choice but to get rid of the food I just ate. The thought of making myself vomit was not appealing to me in the least, but my subconscious programming had me backed into a corner; I truly felt like I had no choice. Forcing myself to vomit was not easy, nor glamorous, but I was an expert at disassociating from my body. When I was finished, I had this huge rush of relief come over me. I felt like I could breathe again. I felt like a giant wave of rage had just been flushed down the toilet. In that moment of euphoria, I was calm. It wasn't long until I was addicted to this behavior, just to get to "calm."

The next decade pushed me even more beyond my emotional limits. Just as my mother was coping better, I was diagnosed with breast cancer. At this point in my life, I had the support of a life partner and our amazing dogs. After deep soul searching, I realized that I needed to answer that lifelong whispering of my soul: I wanted to help heal animals.

Over the next three years, between numerous surgeries, I attended the *Healing Touch for Animals* workshops. For the first time in my life, I started to truly feel alive with a purpose. I received my practitioner certification after countless hours working on shelter animals. My life finally felt perfect. I was honoring my body and soul and believed my eating disorder was cured.

As my health improved, my mother started to "need" me again, my stress levels skyrocketed, and my numbing habits returned. That intense year ended with losing my home in a major hurricane and my brother Bill to suicide. Once again, I was the emotional support person/grief counselor for my mom despite all of my own personal grief and loss.

I continued to practice Animal Communication and Healing, and once our local animal shelter reopened, I returned to give and receive healing from all of the animals. It was during this time that I recalled my childhood days of connecting with shelter dogs, exchanging stories, and dreaming about having a sanctuary for dogs.

I am especially fond of senior dogs and dogs with special needs. I've dedicated my volunteer services to a few special needs dogs over the years. The last one was a beautiful eight-year-old German Shepherd by the name of Payton Rose.

Payton Rose had a hard life and came into the shelter in poor physical, mental, and emotional health. I fell in love with her immediately and couldn't wait to assist with her healing process.

But our daily routine came to an abrupt halt as the world faced a global pandemic and everything shut down. Volunteers were not allowed at the shelter, and foster homes were found for many of the animals. Payton did not get fostered.

A month prior to the national lockdown my relationship with my life partner ended. I went into this pandemic feeling alone and depressed, like so many others. Thankfully, I was finally in my own apartment with my loving and supportive dogs, Skylar and Merlin. I spent the next three months diving deep into self-reflection and my own healing. I started working with two different life coaches. Specifically, my mindset coach truly helped me rise above my depression and question my fifty-year-old belief system. Through consistent self-work and introspection, I realized that I could still pursue my lifelong dreams, and the idea of my sanctuary for dogs solidified.

After three months in national lockdown, I was allowed back in the shelter to resume my care of Payton Rose. We were overjoyed to see each other again, but I noticed a marked decline in her health as the stress of being in a shelter environment had weighed down her spirit.

For months, I would visit with Payton daily, even if for only five minutes, depending on my schedule. Despite my best attempts to help her relax and heal, her physical and emotional challenges continued. She was an extremely talkative girl and had so much to say to me. Her daily sermons were very direct and delivered with conviction. After every one of her speeches, I would say, "Payton, I promise you that after I see you through your journey, I will start the sanctuary."

As the months passed, she continued to deteriorate, despite care and an abundance of love from me. After much contemplation and many discussions with the vet, the director of the shelter decided that the kindest thing to do was to euthanize her. This decision crushed my heart, but deep down I knew that Payton's physical body was no longer able to serve her great spirit. The director granted me permission to adopt my sweet girl and take her to my vet for a private euthanasia.

When Payton's special day arrived, I had a party for her which included swimming, playing with her favorite toys, and eating all of her favorite foods. Two of my dear friends, who knew and loved Payton, joined in the celebration. We took turns telling her how amazing she was and how grateful we were to be in her life. Payton listened intently to every word while tilting her head from side to side as she feasted on pancakes, waffles, bananas, and peanut butter. As her appointment time grew near, she made things easy on me. She jumped off the lounge chair, ran over to the fence, and started jumping up and barking at my truck. Payton was ready.

The vet had a large blanket laid out on the floor so I could lay with her and talk her through the process. After the sedation kicked in she finally laid down and rested her head in my arms. As I pressed my lips against her face, I could feel my tears running down her fur. Just as he started injecting into her vein I was whispering my promises in her ear. I immediately heard, "Thank you, mom. I love you," and within an instant, I felt her enormous spirit leave her body. My Payton Rose was finally at peace. Her tired, beautiful body laid perfectly still in my arms and her eyes were closed, something I had never witnessed in eleven months. I took a deep breath and beyond my sadness, I felt a deep sense of peace in my soul.

It was because of my experience with this beautiful girl that "Payton's Promise" was born. Payton's Promise is a nonprofit organization that provides sanctuary for homeless dogs that are nearing end of life, who have special needs, or are otherwise difficult to adopt. Our dogs under hospice care can comfortably live out their lives with us while receiving deep love and respect. Our nonterminal dogs receive whatever care is necessary with the same love and respect. These dogs are often available for adoption to loving humans who resonate with our mission.

Since following my soul's calling, I am finally honoring myself.

# PATH TO YOUR POWER

## MY WHOLEHEARTED MESSAGE TO YOU

The best guidance I can offer is to start with finding a qualified therapist or life coach who listens with an open heart and genuinely hears you. I changed therapists many times during my adult years simply because we didn't feel aligned, and that's okay! You will know when you find the right person who will help you grow. You will feel it deep in your soul. As a result of dedicated self-care, I've learned a few things that I hope will assist you in reconnecting with your beautiful soul.

Perfection is a lie. I believed the key to happiness and success was having the "perfect" life: the perfect relationship, body, and career without struggle. However, I found myself struggling extensively in all three areas. The more I focused on perfectionism and looking for external validation, the more my internal conflicts intensified.

You can still struggle and evolve at the same time. Once I began my healing journey, I gave myself permission to be me, and look for love and acceptance from within. As I started to finally confront my inner critic, I realized that our personal evolution is on a continuum. There will be struggles. It's learning how to work through the struggles with self-compassion and grace that is the true key to happiness and success.

Any low self-esteem you experience is not your fault. It is simply faulty programming instilled in us unknowingly from the adults in our life who believed they were doing their best to raise us. This pattern is often generational. The good news is that we can rewire our brains and change our belief systems.

Finally, lean into the deepest desire of your heart and soul. It's never "too late" to start something new or ignite a passion that was buried so long ago. You're not "too young" or "too old" to nourish your soul. The only time we can truly experience is in the present moment, so try to stay there, being present with yourself. Most importantly, your healing journey doesn't need to be anywhere near perfect. Embrace your imperfections and know that you are exactly where you're supposed to be. Know that every experience in your life brought you exactly to where you are today. Start where you are and move forward with gratitude, one step at a time. Many blessings to you, dear one. You are loved and supported.

## ABOUT

Karen Thomas is a registered nurse with nearly 30 years of experience who combines western medicine with energy work and holistic methods to help homeless, abandoned dogs with medical needs. As the founder of Payton's Promise, a nonprofit organization that provides a sanctuary for dogs in need, she has found her true passion and life calling. You can learn more at https://PawsitiveTouch.org/.

When Karen isn't saving a puppy or helping a hospice dog cross over the rainbow bridge, you can find her jogging through her neighborhood, biking to the beach, swimming in the ocean, playing with essential oils and magical rocks, or standing upside down in a challenging yoga pose.

## CHAPTER 3

# HEALING FROM THE INSIDE OUT BY ERIN ARNETT

*Family disfunction struggles helped define a quest for healing the inner child and creating a life of independence and fulfillment previously unimaginable. Finally coming out of hiding leads to a life of leadership and massive success.*

"Wonder why she is calling me today?" I ask myself as I glance at the caller ID and see that my mom is on the line. I am caught off guard as the first words out of her mouth are, "We need to talk."

It is not unusual for my mom to contact me, but this call's tone is very different. It's not that we do not speak. We never speak *this* way.

Mom struggles to find her words. There is an awkward silence. After what seemed like several minutes, she finally says, "I need to ask you a question." Following another long pause, she asks if my grandfather (her father) had ever been inappropriate with me. The air and space between us is heavy and tense. I am confused, to say the least, and unsure what she is referring to.

I answer "No." In my usual fashion, I am ready to move on with my day . . . almost. A nagging voice in my head tells me to do something that I rarely do. Speak up. After a few moments of silence, I swallow hard and ask the difficult question. "Why?"

My grandfather was a prestigious member of the community. He was a leader in our church, and I looked up to him my entire life. My grandmother was kind and nurturing to others, but was not pleasant to me. My grandfather was always the kind one, or so I thought.

This is how I discovered that, throughout my mom's childhood, my grandfather abused her sexually. She had carried this silent scream her entire life. Now, even as she tried to share it, the words were still stifled. The fact that she'd even called me let me know she was really hurting and struggling; it was incredible.

My feelings usually stay subdued, but not this time; they came flooding in and washing over me. I was in a state of confusion and wasn't sure how to feel. My feelings swayed from disbelief to shock and dismay. Over the following days and weeks, my feelings bubbled up to the surface and continued to overwhelm me.

How could he have done those horrible things? How could he rip away all the wholesomeness and innocence from my mom? Why was it kept a secret for so long? Why did no one speak up? Why now?

Mom was never there for me emotionally. We were not close. I did not confide in her, and we did not talk often. Because of how she raised me, we grew further and further apart after I became an adult.

My childhood is not easy to explain. I come from a large family that was deeply religious. We were poor, but always had food on the table. We had a roof over our heads, yet we were never taught how to take care of it, or ourselves. We were never shown affection or taught to meet our goals. We were sheltered and did not know how to function in everyday society. We did not venture far from home; we only attended church and school and not much else.

In such a large family, my mom rarely worked outside of the home, but at the same time, we were left to our own devices with minimal supervision. There were nominal consequences for our actions, and if anything was brought to my mom's attention, we were shamed for it, and it was never resolved. A typical scenario would be that when my brother would steal my money, I would tell my mom. Her simple response was that I should give her my money, then it wouldn't be stolen. Unfortunately, this was not a unique scenario in our home, and it happened often.

At a very early age, I learned to stay quiet and not cause any problems. My mom mistook this for strength and independence and, years later, I realized that she felt that I didn't need her help. But that never stopped me from wanting her love and affection.

I do not remember experiencing much joy or happiness, and I did not smile much. I grew increasingly introverted and sunk further into the shadows. For as long as I attended school, I received good grades, but I lost interest and never completed high school. Up to this point in my life, I had never strived to accomplish anything and did not do much. I never participated in sports, I never had many friends, and I never ventured far from home.

After this conversation with mom, I spent a long time thinking and taking a long hard look at myself. I looked at my husband and our children; I looked at our house and the life that we had built. I finally realized that I was in the same marriage my parents were in. One where mom stayed home, and dad worked. It was more of a roommate situation with no genuine partnership, care, or intimacy. I was not showing up for my marriage or my kids.

I decided I did not want to continue that way. I did not want to live an empty life and continue passing down this pain that was given to me. I did not want anyone else to experience the pain that I had experienced as a child, the yearning for love and not receiving it.

I wanted to change and be there for my husband, and I wanted to find that spark and joy again. In all of the ways my mom wasn't there for me, I wanted to be there for my children, not only physically, but also emotionally. It was increasingly important to me that my kids grow up knowing I loved them since I'd grown up without love from my mother. I wanted to make sure that they felt my love every day of their life. I decided to change my perspective and be a better person for myself and then for my husband and children.

Unfortunately, my journey did not go as expected. Unbeknownst to me, my husband was deep down the rabbit hole of drug addiction. Many behaviors go along with addiction, none of which make for a good marriage. For those who have never experienced what this is like, our world was turned upside down very slowly over time. It was so gradual that I didn't recognize it was happening. The lies and deception were endless. On the financial front, monies were lost and never replaced, bills didn't get paid, and our credit was ruined. Our lives were slowly destroyed, all while the person I loved and trusted the most was smiling at me and telling me that everything was okay.

The path of self-discovery was not easy. I had no money, my ex-husband was deep into his drug addiction, and I was on my own. I continued my journey as I moved from the big city to a small coastal town where life was much slower. I worked hard to create a life for myself. I took an active role in raising my children. I volunteered at their schools, coached their sports, and was present for them. I took a very different role than the ones modeled by my family when no one ever showed up for me.

After my divorce, I faced the daunting task of learning how to function in society. Since I was never taught this as a child, I was very introverted and awkward. I was never taught to look someone in the eye when speaking to them or how to shake someone's hand and say hello. It was an agonizing task, and I often found myself feeling very self-conscious. I felt like that small child again, and if I spoke up or showed enthusiasm, it would be beaten out of me as it had been by my siblings. This made me want to sink even further into the shadows. I never spoke up and rarely gave my opinion. I always felt like I would say the wrong thing and that others were judging me. So, I sat in the back of the room and let others do the talking.

Following that eventful conversation with my mom, I worked hard at bettering myself. I found a good therapist (many over the years, in fact) and learned to set healthy boundaries. It feels like I have read every self-help book there is and watched every Ted Talk on shame and guilt. My mom passed her shame and guilt down to me, and I wore it like a heavy set of chains. With all that had happened, I had the daunting task of slowly learning to let those chains go, how to take life by force, and finally be free.

I have come a long way since that day. It feels like a lifetime ago. I can remember the day when I knew that I was finally learning to find my voice. As usual, I was sitting at the back of a meeting, listening to someone else speak. Except this time, I spoke up. It was a knee-jerk reaction; I did it without realizing what I was doing and without overthinking it. Without hesitation, I was thanked, and the meeting continued. What happened? What had I done? What was this feeling? The feeling was confidence. I had found my voice; it had come on suddenly and quickly. I wasn't ashamed; I was elegant and had spoken my mind. I couldn't believe what had happened, and it felt good.

Years later, I learned that my mom, like her mom, had an autoimmune disease. Like many things in our home, this was rarely mentioned. If the topic was brought up, there were brief and short answers without much explanation. Much to my surprise, I was also diagnosed with the same auto-immune disease, and I was not about to let it beat me. I saw doctor after doctor until I found the right one. After some adjustments, I have learned to eat healthily and exercise, and I have been able to keep most of my symptoms at bay.

One of the side effects of this self-discovery journey is healing myself on the inside and the outside. Not surprisingly, my doctor's "go-to" for me has always been to prescribe anti-depressants and anti-anxiety medication. As I continued to work on myself, my mental health and my physical health improved. Years of therapy taught me that holding onto my past will cause physical illness as well.

Since my mom's passing, my father and I have become closer. He is one of my closest friends. We now have a bond that I always wanted as a child but could never put into words. Our relationship continues to grow stronger as we learn to navigate this new connection. It, too, has its ups and downs, but we are learning how to grow our new bond.

My journey of healing myself from the inside out continues today. I work on myself every day, and I'm learning more and more every day how to find my voice and speak louder. It will always be a struggle, but it's a struggle that I look forward to facing. I will never go back to being the person I used to be. I often reflect on her, but have made peace with my past. I still have my good and bad days, but I persevere.

The sky is the limit now. I have finally learned to shed the chains that once held me back, and I'm learning to get rid of the straps that once bound me. There will always be work to do, but I am at a point where the little Erin inside me is now happy and feels safe to speak out.

## PATH TO YOUR POWER

### MENDING YOUR BROKEN CHILD WITHIN

One of the most important things I've learned is that if we don't take time to heal our inner child, then all of the "adult" healing is mostly a waste of time. If you are in a place right now where you are looking for a different way to heal from past wounds and pain, here is my "recipe" for moving forward to heal. These steps should be followed in order.

Forgive yourself. Forgiving ourselves is the foundation to moving forward from our past. Once we *decide* to forgive, the hard work is done. Choosing to do this is the hardest part. We, as women, want to feel a certain way before we are willing to forgive ourselves. When in reality, we receive that feeling once we forgive ourselves.

Learn how to breathe. So many times, we forget to breathe. Have you ever felt anxious? If so, then guess what? You're not breathing. Long deep breaths have a very calming effect. When you feel anxious, sit and take a couple of long and deep breaths. It will not relieve your anxiety, but it will help.

Stop taking on the world. We have all experienced anxiety, felt like we are floundering or spinning. As women, we believe that we have to take on the world head-on. We think that we are weak if we ask for help. The reality is it is much harder to ask for (and receive) help from others than most will admit. There are people in the world who know more than we do. We need to lean on them so they can help us in our journey.

Make peace with the past. This is an essential step. We cannot move forward until we have looked back. The past is what defines us, until it doesn't anymore. We need to make peace with our past so that we can stop repeating it and move forward.

Get outside and move. Besides the fact that the sun allows us to produce vitamin D, physical health significantly increases mental health. This step is a reward and will only serve to improve your self-love.

## ABOUT

Erin Arnett is an experienced Real Estate Appraiser in the Florida Keys, tech nerd, maker of silly t-shirts and anything with glitter, and an entrepreneur running three businesses. Having recently returned to college, she is finally fulfilling a long-life goal of earning her degree. She is a member of many community organizations and enjoys donating her time and talents. Soon she will step into the role of president of one of these organizations, a far cry from that little girl terrified to speak up. Erin's newest venture, Pearls of Wisdom, helps business owners expand authentically so that they can experience their greatest joy and wealth. To learn more, visit www.PearlsOfWisdomByErin.com or email Erin at info@pearlsofwisdombyerin.com.

The mother of two daughters who are grown and have families of their own, Erin has repaired her family relationships, which are now closer than ever. She also has an ever-expanding circle of friends. When she is not engaged in her business ventures, she enjoys volunteering, spending time at the gym, and hanging out with her crew watching football and thinking up brilliant new sayings for her silly t-shirts.

# NOTES AND REFLECTIONS

## CHAPTER 4

# RAINBOW AFTER THE STORM BY REBECCA WEIKEL

*A letter to dad helps resolve feelings of grief and guilt lingering decades after his death. Hitting rock bottom and asking for help allows us to begin to see clear skies above.*

It's six in the morning, the sun is starting to rise, birds are beginning to chirp, and I hear the words from the aide I have been dreading to hear: "Girls, it's time." I race up the stairs with my sister to be at his bedside. My dad had already taken his last breath and now all I could do was hold his hand until his heart stopped beating. I said a prayer as his heart took its last beat and watched as my dad left this earth.

A whirlwind of feelings came over me. First, the relief that almost a year after my dad's diagnosis of pancreatic cancer, his suffering was finally over. Then, the panic that my dad has died and now I don't know what I am going to do. Who am I going to call when my car breaks down and I need help? Who will join me and talk about baseball games and Auburn football? Then came the anxiety of having to pick up the phone and call my mom about him dying.

That phone call was one of the hardest calls I have ever had to make. Telling my mother that the father of her children has passed away was heart breaking. I can't imagine what she was thinking. She not only had to be there for my sister and me, but also go through the grief of losing him. After that phone call, all I wanted to do was pack up my bag and go home. Being exhausted both emotionally and physically, I desperately needed to be surrounded by the love and comfort of my mom and to have the space to process my loss privately.

But it wasn't that easy. My dad's wife had called the hospice nurse to come and then the funeral home director came to take my dad away. When everything was done, I thought I could finally go home. But instead, my sister and I had to go pick out clothes for my dad's viewing and go to the church to finalize the logistics of the funeral service. I was numb, keeping my emotions held in while going through the physical motions of what had to be done.

I remember getting into my sister's car after we were done with the walk through at the church, feeling a sense of release. Now **finally** I could allow myself to experience all the emotions that I had been feeling over the past week while my dad was in hospice care. Instead, glancing at my phone as I lowered myself into the seat, I was faced with a text message expressing condolences for our loss. How did she know? Only a few hours had passed between the time my dad left us and now. My sister and I had only spoken to our mom.

I soon discovered a post had been made on Facebook about my dad losing his battle to cancer. I was mad. My sister and I had just lost our father; we had barely enough time to process everything; and now the whole world knew what had happened.

Then a panic set in. We had not yet had a chance to call my dad's aunt and uncle, who my dad thought of as second parents. We prayed that they had not seen the news on Facebook. Thankfully they had been out of town, and we were able to talk to them before they saw it, which was a huge relief. No one should discover that their nephew has died by reading a Facebook post.

The days after my dad's death I felt like I was in a fog. I had to make essential decisions about his funeral and where he was to be buried; all while trying to get everything together for the closing on my new townhome. Yep, that's right, I was in the process of buying a house! In fact, I closed on it two weeks after my father had passed away.

That time in my life was supposed to be fun and exciting, but instead, the thought that my dad was never going to see where I lived was eating away at me inside. I didn't even want to think about how I was going to decorate my new home, and in reality, I just wanted to blink my eyes and have everything done for me. But that's not reality. Instead, I slowly moved my things out of my mother's house and into my new home because I was afraid of being in a new place all alone with my thoughts, feelings, and fears. My biggest fear was that I was going to move into my home by myself and sink into a deep depression over the death of my dad.

Unfortunately, my biggest fear came true. After taking a month off work to mourn and release the anxiety I had been feeling from the loss of my father, I returned to my job as a registered nurse. I still remember getting into the elevator and as I got closer to the unit I worked on, taking a deep breath and saying to myself, "conceal, don't feel." These words from the movie, *Frozen*, were the words I had said to myself every morning while my father was going through his cancer battle. Those words brought comfort to me during that stormy period of my life. I said them because all I wanted to do was get through my twelve-hour shifts without crying or breaking down. My patients deserved a nurse that was 100% focused on their care and wellbeing.

For the next few months, I would say those same words to myself every time I went to work. It got me through the days, especially the ones where I was taking care of patients that had a history of pancreatic cancer or just cancer in general. That was until one Friday night in December close to Christmas.

I was sitting on my couch, looking at the two-foot tree I had bought and decorated, and thought to myself, *I can't do this anymore. I can't live my life without my father. It's too hard. It would be so easy to end this heartache, and not have to deal with it anymore. I could easily go upstairs to my room right now, take a handful of Advil, and just go to sleep and never wake up*. But then the thought of putting my mom and sister through that sank in. *I couldn't do that to them. It would kill them.* As all these thoughts came rushing into my head, tears began to drip down my face. I knew I had hit rock bottom and I needed help.

I had an appointment with my doctor a few days after Christmas, so I decided to wait until then to speak with her about all of the emotions I had been feeling. During that appointment, I expressed how I was having a hard time with my father's death and asked if she had any recommendations. She suggested I speak with a counselor, then gave me the name of a local practice she often refers patients to.

After the appointment, I spoke to my mom about the struggle I was having with my father's death and shared that I'd received a referral to a counselor to help me with my grief. She agreed getting help was a good idea, so I went home and looked into the practice. Going through the bios of everyone there, I couldn't find one that I thought I could really click with and feel comfortable enough to open up to.

Then I decided to look for counselors through my health insurance; still no luck. It was at that point I was starting to feel helpless.

It wasn't until I met my mom and sister for lunch one afternoon that I found someone who could help me. Her name was Allyson Roberts. My mom had taken one of her classes and thought it might be a good idea for my sister and me to enroll in Allyson's *Unapologetic Power* class. It took me a split second to come to a decision. I was in!

When I first started that class, I was an emotional wreck. During my first meeting with Allyson, I couldn't hold back the tears and hurt that I was feeling; I was so embarrassed. Here I was, sitting down with a person I had never met, crying over the littlest things she would ask me. But, after that meeting and many wet tissues, I began to feel a slight sense of relief. I had found the person who was going to help me navigate this storm that I had found myself in.

After my father passed away, I had many negative thoughts about how I wish I had done more to help him. As a nurse, I felt helpless. I wanted my father to get better so bad and it was hard to accept that there was nothing I could do. The thought, *If I had only done this he would have gotten better*, would creep into my mind. But when working with Allyson over the next few months, I learned how to change my thought process about things.

The negative thoughts I would say to myself slowly began to disappear. Every time I had a negative thought in my head I would say to myself, "STOP! I'm not going to think this way anymore because it's not true. I did nothing wrong." This way of thinking has completely changed things in my life. I was no longer "doom and gloom" about everything I was going through. Instead, I was starting to feel happier and could look at the bright side of things. My storm clouds were turning to partly cloudy skies.

Once the class was over, I knew I still had plenty of work to do. So I continued to work with Allyson both in group classes and one-on-one sessions. During those sessions, I was able to work through the grief I was experiencing with the loss of my dad. In fact, the one piece of advice I got from Allyson that completely changed my grieving process was to write a letter to my dad. The letter needed to include everything I had been feeling about my dad. Then, when I was done, I needed to burn it. This would allow me to get everything off my chest and finally release it.

My father wasn't always around while I was growing up. He was out of town on business throughout the week and when he was home, he wasn't "home." He was either out playing his guitar on Saturday nights at a restaurant to earn extra money for his pilot's license or spending time with his friends. He missed out on a lot of important things in my life, which led to a lot of heartache while I was growing up. I've never understood why my dad constantly chose his friends over spending time with his family.

Yet, when my dad was home and engaged, he was amazing. He coached my softball teams and when he wasn't traveling, took me to my batting and pitching lessons. I have such fond memories with my dad teaching me all about softball/baseball. I can still remember my dad putting tape on a bucket of softballs the night before our first practice so he could teach my softball team how to throw properly. Something so simple, but it changed the way I played the whole game.

When I began writing that letter to my dad, thoughts and emotions began to pour out of me. I was writing things I had felt when I was a kid, things I had held in my entire life. I was also writing about feelings no one knew I had. My younger self was finally getting a voice about the things she experienced and felt. When I finished writing the letter, I felt so much lighter. It felt like a weight was lifted off my shoulders. I no longer had to carry those feelings around. That was the moment I started to see sunlight. I was finally starting to get out of the storm.

To help with my grief, I also turned to listening to music my dad used to play on his guitar. My dad loved playing his guitar. In fact, he used to play every night when he got home from work. He exposed me to all different types of music, but probably my favorite was from the Beatles. My dad loved the Beatles. He would play every song from "A Hard Day's Night" to "Here Comes the Sun." After my dad passed away, I changed my alarm clock to that song because it made me feel closer to him. I get to wake up to that song every morning and feel a sense of peace. I know that my dad is with me every day.

But even though I have been able to move forward, my grieving process is definitely not over. My grief comes in waves. One moment I am fine while driving home from work, and the next moment, I'm sitting at a stop light crying because I am looking at a restaurant I use to go to with my dad. I am also still working through the realization that my dad will never see my home. For over half a year, I didn't want to do things to fix up my house. The plan was that my dad was going to help me, but it never came to fruition. Instead, it took help from Allyson and a push from my mom to finally start getting pictures hung on my walls and my office redecorated.

Everyone goes through the grieving process differently; it isn't an easy process. Some go through the stages of grief quickly, while for others, it can take a long time. I was in a dark hole when my father passed away. I didn't know or see how I would ever get through this. In fact, it wasn't until I hit my rock bottom and asked for help, that I could begin to see a blue sky and a rainbow. Sometimes when we are in the middle of a storm, we feel helpless and can't imagine ever seeing a rainbow again. We have gone through these storms so regularly that we keep our guard up, waiting for the next storm to hit while often missing the blue skies and rainbow above us. That's why asking for help is so important. Having an objective person help navigate the grief you are feeling can help you see those blue skies and rainbows.

I now use that little bit of blue sky to raise money for the Pancreatic Cancer Action Network (PanCAN) through participating in their PurpleStride event every year. PurpleStride helps raise money for PanCAN, which then helps fund research that covers everything from early detection to new treatment options. They also provide information to patients about the different treatment options, what type of diet you should have, and any other support resources a pancreatic cancer patient may need. I wish I'd known about this organization while my dad was fighting his battle. This is why I am so passionate about it. I don't want anyone else to have to go through what I went through.

The important thing with grief is, don't be afraid to feel your feelings and ask for help if you need it. If I hadn't taken time off from work when my dad passed away, listened to all the music he loved, started working with Allyson Roberts, written a letter telling him how I felt, or become involved with an organization that changes lives, I don't know where I would be today. Losing a parent is hard. But I want you to have hope that you will get through it, and you are not alone.

## NOTES AND REFLECTIONS

## PATH TO YOUR POWER

### FIND YOUR OWN BLUE SKY

Don't be afraid to seek and find the help you need. It's crucial for you to see your path through the eyes of someone who is not a relative or a friend, but an objective person trained to lead you through your pain.

Be open to trying new things. Write. Scream. Cry. Walk. Meditate. Listen to music. It doesn't matter how you get there, but you won't arrive at a different place on your path if you keep doing the same thing over and over again.

Change your self-talk. You probably speak to yourself in a way you'd never dream of talking to someone you love, or maybe even a complete stranger. Learn to reframe your thoughts and your language so that you are kinder and gentler with yourself.

Give yourself grace. Don't compare yourself to others. If it is taking you longer to recover from a huge loss, it's okay. You have permission to walk on your journey at your own pace.

Find a cause. Fighting against the cancer that killed my dad helps me feel like I'm making a difference. While your cause doesn't have to be directly related to what you're going through, donating your time and/or money to a non-profit that is near and dear to your heart will help you heal.

## ABOUT

Rebecca Weikel holds a Bachelor of Science degree in Health Services Administration from Auburn University and a Bachelor of Science in Nursing from Chamberlain University. Her internship in Moshi, Tanzania, where she worked in a HIV/Aids clinic at the local hospital, taught her much about the human connection and treatment process for combating HIV/Aids. She is as an advocate for the Red Campaign that raises money for the Global Fund to combat Aids, Tuberculosis, and Malaria in African countries. Currently serving as a registered nurse in Atlanta, she is planning to continue her education so that she can have an even deeper connection with her patients locally and around the world.

In her spare time, Rebecca enjoys traveling the world and learning about different cultures and societies. Her goal is to reach all seven continents and she's only two continents away from reaching that goal. She is also interested in using travel and her nursing experience to help care for people who are suffering from various medical conditions around the world. In the fall she spends most of her weekends cheering on her Auburn Tigers Football team. When she is not traveling or going to football games, Rebecca is spending time with her family and taking care of her dog, Jack, and cat, Nellie.

# CHAPTER 5

# HEART WALK BY ANN LALLY

*Honor the deep roots developed through uncertainty and even trauma; they will keep you grounded and able to see the possibilities. From librarian to animal communicator and psychic intuitive, the thirty-year journey that's changing lives.*

I am three years old, and my sister has just been born. My neighbor has gifted me a kitten. I am so happy and excited. This neighbor has lots of cats. I spend lots of time at her house because I love being around cats; they are so fun, so cute, so cuddly. As I sit at the family dinner table, my kitten jumps on the table and my dad, in an act that is regretted to this day, says "Ann, I told you to keep the cat off the table!" He throws the kitten off the table too forcefully, breaking the kitten's back.

I have no memory of what happened next; the incident is never discussed. However, it has a huge and I mean HUGE impact on my life. For decades, I believed the death of the kitten was my fault; that I wasn't worthy of nice things. The one thing that was mine–this tiny, helpless being that I loved–had been killed before my eyes because of something I did. I couldn't trust myself or anyone else because my trust had been betrayed.

I was also subject to emotional abuse, insidious emotional abuse. The kind of abuse that is vaporous, like air, and slowly works its way into your psyche . . . particularly if you are already traumatized. "Oh, you don't want to do that!" "FEET!!! Don't you mean inches???" "You'll be lucky if you get a man." "You could have died!" All of this subtle language — designed to keep me safe, smarten me up, and make me acceptable to my family — resulted in a life of smallness, where I craved security and the known.

All of this honestly could have turned me into a doormat for boyfriends and others to walk all over, but it didn't. There was still a strong light of willfulness and irrepressibility within me. Despite two marriage proposals, I never married because I knew in my heart they would want me to change my essential nature to match their dreams. I wanted life on my terms, not on "our" terms, and I was fucking fighting to get there, even though at times that fighting looked like giving in as I sat and waited for guidance from Spirit.

In 1989 I failed my Master's exams and fell into a deep depression, so much so that I ended up in therapy. I worked hard there, learning to trust my intuition — which I had shoved aside when I was three and my kitten was killed — and understanding how to trust myself to make significant life changes based on my intuition.

I learned that because of the early trauma, my energy field had become porous, and thus, I was more sensitive to the world around me. This extreme sensitivity and inability to deal with it caused me to shut down this part of myself. As I gained confidence in my intuition, I understood that although I had shoved it aside, it was far better at life decisions than my brain was. I also knew that IF I listened to it, it would never lead me down the wrong path.

Because I was trying to figure out my next step in life, I read *What Color is Your Parachute* by Richard Bowles. This book helped me see that because my favorite activity in graduate school was research — both doing my own and helping people do theirs–that being a librarian would be a perfect career for me. It felt right. I was excited; in fact, this career was so divinely guided that my graduate school application was immediately accepted with an offer to be a paid teaching assistant. I enjoyed the classes, the teaching, and working at the reference desk — this was the job for me!

As I worked my way through the library profession, I had a very particular career trajectory — I wanted to do digital library work. When I was offered a job doing this work at the University of Washington, I was over the moon excited to move to Seattle and start my new job.

The early days were fun as I learned what the organization needed and started making proposals for change. Nobody liked my ideas (although they had when I interviewed for the job) and pushed back; eventually people stopped listening to me. I continued beating my head against this brick wall because I loved living in Seattle. The climate was perfect for me, and I enjoyed the landscape.

By the time I landed in Seattle, I had worked in two other libraries, always leveling up and learning new skills to support my dream career trajectory. Now I had achieved that dream title, and theoretically my dream life, but I realized it wasn't really what I wanted. I was done being a librarian and had moved so many times I wasn't interested in moving again. So here I was in a job I didn't like in a place I loved, knowing deep in my soul I was where I was supposed to be. I worked very hard to acquire the security and comforts I craved, including health insurance and tenure (i.e. job security), but that security, while keeping me safe, was also slowly suffocating me to death.

I took up knitting as something to do in the evenings and one day it hit me . . . this is what the rest of my life looks like… working… knitting… working… knitting. This is life?!

I had trusted my intuition implicitly for years and knew I had been divinely guided to this place, but now I was moldering in a chair, stuck on an endless hamster wheel of boredom and ennui. I knew I hadn't "gone down the wrong path," and yet, I couldn't seem to figure out the next stage.

It didn't help that I went into menopause early, so in addition to the boredom, I was having hot flashes and crying all the time, only sleeping two hours a night, and freaking out in my doctor's office because I was old and would be alone for the rest of my life. Every once in a while I would ask my guides, "Why is this happening?!!" The response was, "You have something important to do in ten years and we can't have you going through this then; you need to be finished sooner." I would then ask, "Well, what is it I will be doing?" "You'll see." *Sigh.*

I was once again in my therapist's office crying about how I was old, and no one wanted to be my friend, let alone boyfriend, and everything was over for me. My therapist had finally had enough of my whining. She looked me in the eye and said, "Ann, you're 44 not 84, GET IT TOGETHER." 2008 was the year I decided I needed to get my life together and be the captain of my boat rather than simply existing.

Did I? No.

It took another two years to finally get me off the couch.

There wasn't one big moment when I decided I needed to deprogram myself, to live my life with purpose and intent, doing what I loved rather than what was expected of me. It was a series of small moments, based in quiet desperation, that built up to the point where I simply could not continue on as I was.

One of the tools I used to deprogram myself from playing small was a "heart walk" session. A heart walk is when a practitioner journeys within a client's energetic heart to discover messages that offer a new perspective regarding the client's personal happiness and sense of purpose. The practitioner was in a light trance and told me many things about my younger self. Actually, she reminded me of many things I was interested in when I was younger. At one point she said, "I see you at about six years old. You're holding one of those pens with a big feather on it and you're telling me you're a poet. You write about flowers and animals. You know poetry is an expression of the soul. You also say you're a healer."

I was quite buoyed by this and was interested in what she would see next. As she moved deeper into my heart, she said, "I see a heavy pair of oak doors. OK, now the doors are opening and there is a beautiful ice crystal that looks like a snowflake." I was . . . appalled is the best word I have. She was perfectly professional and had no judgement around this, but I certainly did. My heart was protected by heavy oak doors and if someone managed to get past these, they'd encounter an ice crystal.

I had to go digging, again and deeper, to uncover the cause of the over-protected heart. I owed it to the poet and healer — the irrepressible one — to do the work of healing.

Around the same time as the heart walk, I was (finally) demoted at work, given a different job, and moved to a dank, airless cubicle in a department filled with energy vampires. It was, in some ways, a relief; I could stop beating my head against a wall while people ignored me; I didn't have to fight for my department's (and its employees') relevance; and I could disappear into a world of books.

But the lighting was terrible, the people worse, and the job mind-numbingly dull.

In 2016 I made an appointment with an intuitive I had been following online for ten years. The session was like a gift from God. I knew I was a psychic intuitive and had some skills that would benefit others, but I didn't know what to do with them and how they could help me begin a different career. One of the first things out of her mouth was, "Well, you're clearly a very gifted animal communicator."

I thought to myself, *I am?*

She also said that when some people approach their second Saturn return (around the age of 58 with it affecting your life for a couple of years before and after) the soul starts calling for a life of more purpose and meaning. This session helped calm me down and give me a focus: I was going to study animal communication! I did and I loved it! It was a way to put my skills to work to help animals and people and to be of service.

I thought, this — animal communication — was going to be my ticket out of the library. I was still so desperate to leave. As you, dear reader, likely know, desperation is not a way to start a business. Nevertheless, I persisted. The act of learning how to grow a business made me appreciate the money my day job offered so that I could be calm and deliberate about how to grow my business. My 9 to 5 fueled my love of animal communication and gave me the space to learn how to be an entrepreneur while helping to calm my brain down a bit. My vocation was the thing that supported my avocation.

However, there was still much work to do. I needed to "get my mind right." I could see that I had blocks around being out on my own as an entrepreneur, showing up as an animal communicator and psychic intuitive to others (i.e. being a weirdo) in order to promote my business, and just generally having more confidence to put myself out there to the world.

Looking back on the last thirty years since I learned to trust my intuition and decided to become a librarian, I can see the path that got me here. I was learning different skills, how to trust myself, express myself; how to get up in front of an audience and talk — about literally anything — at a moment's notice. Budgeting, supervising staff, and how to work one-on-one with people are all skills that I have learned thanks to being a librarian. So, you see, as I knew all along, my intuition wasn't wrong, I just needed patience. Patience to see the next step, patience to trust my intuition.

Along my journey I reached out to others — psychics, therapists, shamans — to help me identify what was happening and where I had blind spots regarding my soul's growth. All of these encounters helped me see things from a different angle or see something that was holding me back that I could only identify with an impartial person.

My personal journey was unique. I am grateful for the people along the way who offered an alternative perspective. At the end of the day, however, it was up to me to dig deep, get my fingernails dirty and do the hard work of making peace with my past so I could move into my future with excitement and joy.

While I was looking through old journals in preparation for writing this chapter, I ran across this passage from 2011: "One of our assignments for class is to write a thank you note to ourselves. When I think about what I want to write, what overwhelmingly comes up for me is that I am so thankful I haven't given up. I know things are fixable and that I can find a solution or a person to help me find the solution. This is true for me on every level. I am just so grateful that I am as willful as I am." This sentiment is as true today as it was in

2011. I am still grateful to myself for not giving up, for being willful and irrepressible, and fucking fighting for my life.

When you plant a sapling, if you fertilize it all the time you deny it the chance to dig deep for nourishment. Those deep roots, if allowed to develop, are what prevent the tree from being uprooted in a windstorm. Those deep roots, developed over years of searching for sustenance, for nourishment, are what ultimately allows the tree a long, healthy, and happy life. Honor the deep roots developed through uncertainty and even trauma; those are what keep you grounded and able to see the possibilities.

The feeling of knowing you're in the right place while still being unhappy is rough. The doubt and uncertainty can leave you questioning your sanity at times. I'm here to tell you this challenge is navigable. You have an irrepressible spirit within you who loves you and is excited to be here. Devote some time to recovering her; she will take your hand and lead you to an amazing life.

## NOTES AND REFLECTIONS

# PATH TO YOUR POWER

## JOURNEY TO YOUR HEART WALK

Here are the five tools that helped me find my way to the things that make my heart sing. May they do the same for you!

Write. Write, write, write, write, write. Write until all of the crap that clouds your heart is out and on a piece of paper. Even if it's just the same old words over and over again. You will eventually get all of that out of the way and get to your heart.

Explore. What grabs your attention? What do you keep seeing and being drawn to? What are you curious about? Follow that.

Breathe. Calming the central nervous system with any kind of breathing exercise can help you access your heart's desire.

Go with the flow. What is it that takes your outside of time? I'm talking here about activities that when you're finished, you find that hours have gone by without you noticing. Social media scrolling doesn't count, by the way.

Embrace nature. Spend time outdoors with the birds, bees, flowers, and trees. "Forest bathing" is a new trend to get people outside and away from the noise and distractions of our day-to-day lives. This closeness with nature can help you hear your heart over the hubbub.

## ABOUT

While Ann Lally is an Animal Communicator, Psychic Intuitive and Wise Woman, she is best known as a Heart Walk Facilitator who holds both individual sessions and intimate retreats. Her ceremonies are designed to help women go from stuck, unhappy, and unable to see a way out to greater clarity on how and where to make changes to improve their lives. Ann's mission in life is to put her clients in touch with dreams and desires of their younger self, before all the outside programming set it in. If you'd like to schedule an individual session, or learn more about the Heart Walk Ceremony retreats, visit www.HeartWalkCeremonies.com.

Ann lives in Edmonds, WA where she gets into mischief with paint, poetry, and friends. You can also find her frolicking on the beach, sitting with her face toward the sun, or dabbling in a little bit of her soul's magic.

# CHAPTER 6

# PASSION AND PURPOSE BY JENNIFER BRIDGES

*Time moves quickly. Don't wait to get on the right path and live your purpose. Honor yourself and look at your past to help shape a brighter future. Happiness and success can return after total devastation.*

Sitting here still numb after the loss of my mom only three weeks ago today, I stare at twelve clocks on my office wall. I'm wondering where the time has gone.

At the same time, I am grateful for the last three-and-a-half years of spending more time with her. I'm also appreciating the lockdown from the pandemic (and break from the hustle of work) allowing me additional quality hours with mom.

Amidst the clocks, displayed on the wall, are these three inspirational quotes that stand out stronger than I've ever noticed them before. It's as if her spirit is here to remind me to keep going as she always did: *1) Follow your dreams, 2) Begin each day as if you had wings*, and, *3) YES*. Thank you, God, for your divine guidance. I'm also thankful for my willingness to listen to You, calling me back home to Alabama from Atlanta, Georgia (my home for twenty-three years) to be with her these years before she passed. For that, I'm deeply grateful.

Sorting through some of my mom's things, I found a quote from the bible that I kept in my wallet. When I moved, I placed it by my computer so I could see it daily, but it was pushed aside over time. It rested in a protective clear cover that had worn over the years.

Although I could now barely read it, I recognized it immediately. I knew it was a "sign" I needed right now, and it hit me right in the heart. *"Anyone who intends to come with me has to let me lead. You're not in the driver's seat – I am. Don't run from suffering, embrace it. Follow me and I'll show you how. Self-help is no help at all; self-sacrifice is the way, my way, to finding yourself, your true self. What good would it do to get everything you want and lose you, the real you?" Luke 9:23-25*

As I sat reliving the cherished memories of my mom as well as my dad who had passed seven years prior, I realized what an impactful and purpose-filled life they had led. No big celebrity status, no huge social media following. They were just two people who lived a simple life in a small town. They loved their family and friends and tried to help others in any way they could.

Thinking of my mom's twenty-seven-year struggle with multiple sclerosis, I realize it wasn't just her struggle. It was our family's; our small family was close. She was fifty-five at the time of her diagnosis; I was thirty. I'm now fifty-six as we lay her to rest at age eighty-one. As I look at the clocks on the wall, I think of my next twenty-seven years and ask myself how I want it to look when my last day is up. I wasn't prepared for what came next as it seems this question hit something deep within me. I heard a whisper deep inside: "Are you following the World's call instead of God's call? Are you trapped in the societal herd (again), blindly pursuing success? What has success cost you?"

You see, some people who know me professionally see me as "successful" because of my professional visibility and business accomplishments. They've somehow concluded that I've got it "going on." But those people who truly know me know that my true success comes from a place much deeper and more personal than my career. In fact, I believe that I only found my true strength when I was at a point of breaking, when I felt the most alone and lost I have ever been. My true power is the strength I discovered when I let go of my desires and opened myself up to the life that was intended for me. In many ways, it was through losing everything that I was able to truly uncover my strength.

My mom was loved by everyone she met, and she was mom to many. More than anyone else I know, she modeled kindness, unconditional love, resilience, perseverance, patience, faith, hope and wisdom. We called her our "Mother Teresa" because she kept the peace among the strong personalities in our family. She supported my sister and me relentlessly. She brought joy and laughter everywhere she went. She loved us with everything in her. Although things were not always perfect, my parents' love shaped my belief in life-long commitment and created a deep-seated devotion to the people I love in life.

It was through these fundamentals and our early foundation that I was able to excel in sports and school. Heading to college, I created a vision for what my life would be. I worked incredibly hard, with my heart set on medical school since ninth grade anatomy class. When we took a field trip to our local medical school, it sealed it for me. Before graduating college and applying to medical school, I met the man I would end up marrying. My vision was clear, my goals were set, and my trajectory was unleashed (or, so I'd thought).

Though I didn't realize it at the time, I had created a vision for the future that would shape the next ten years of my life. So, off I went to pursue my goals.

Of course, life isn't so easily crafted by our own goals. Sometimes life can throw you curve balls that can knock you off even the sturdiest of foundations. Sometimes, life can bring you unexpected and devastating heartbreak, and no matter how hard you work and how determined you are, your plans don't necessarily manifest into your reality. By the age of thirty, everything I had worked for and thought that I wanted, began to unravel.

After college, my marriage took me to a new life, a new job, and a new town four hours away from my family and friends. Things weren't going well from the beginning, and over time, life became worse. My husband was now traveling internationally ninety percent of the time. Not only was I in a new town with no friends, but I was also forced to discontinue my pursuit of medical school in order to make this move with my husband. This meant abandoning a life that was comfortable and thriving, and landing in one of isolation, solitude, and regret.

While I was saddened to leave the professional and independent life I had been creating before our move, my family received devastating news that shook all of us to our core. My mother's illness was, in fact, multiple sclerosis (MS). My small family was a close unit. Just like my parents had always cared for us, my sister and I were determined to help care for our mother.

At the time of my mom's diagnosis, there were only a few doctors in the world who knew, understood, researched, and treated MS. Without treatment, her health rapidly declined. I felt helpless and hopeless. Because of my move, I wasn't home. The doctors didn't know how to treat my mother. I couldn't help her. It was devastating.

The one reprieve I did find at that time was a job that kept me sane and focused. After some time to adjust to my new town, I found work that I loved and new friends that helped me drive away the isolating loneliness. Although I was still far from my mother and dealing with my increasingly difficult marriage, I found some security that helped me feel whole. Looking back, my path to success wasn't a straight line, and my journey hadn't even yet fully begun. Unfortunately, things began to get much worse, before they got better.

After ten years at my corporate job, I moved into what was both a promising and productive career. While my sights were still set on medical school, I discovered a passion for technology and project management that fostered my growth on my career path. Within this space, I found a stability and intentionality that was lacking from the other areas of my life, something I could control while the rest of my world was spiraling out of control.

More and more, I discovered a world that made sense to me, and I began to appreciate the project management role. Perhaps it was because of how disorganized and chaotic the rest of my world felt. But this was a discipline that rewarded organization and expectation. I thrived in this environment, and for a while, it helped keep me sane. It provided security and contentment . . . then things changed.

Our company decided to outsource a significant segment of the workforce as part of a new initiative. Before we could even take it all in, our company announced plans to transition *three thousand* people. While my job was not outsourced, my safety net was replaced with an environment filled with toxicity and stress. Things changed dramatically; many of the remaining employees were fearful and angry. My one reprieve was now my greatest stressor. It was at this time that despair began to truly take over.

I would like to say that the other parts of my life were starting to heal. I'd love to share that my marriage was thriving, and my mother's health was improving. Sadly, it was the opposite, and the culmination of these three areas were a vice grip around my heart. I finally fully plummeted into depression and despair, which was the antithesis of who I was. My happiness and optimism were replaced with a bitter sadness that followed me through my days and sat with me during my isolated nights. I felt I had lost everything that made me who I was, including my goals and dreams, my marriage, my family. I felt alone and stuck. The more I pushed for my version of the future, the worse things got.

I chose to let go of the forces that were driving me in order to listen to the true desires of my heart. I stopped and journeyed inward to meet the pain, embrace the disappointment, explore the mess, and discover the gems. It was time to listen to my soul that was screaming for freedom. Instead of praying (desperately begging) that God fulfill "my will, my way," I humbly asked Him to show me "his will, his way." I had to ask the hard questions about who I was (and was not). I had to admit some difficult truths about myself and about my marriage.

In the end, the things I was striving for were not in alignment with the woman I had become. I knew then that the pieces of my life I was clinging to were the pieces that I needed to let go. Deep within, I had a new vision for my future. One that would empower me to become the woman I am today, not the woman I was still trying to be in a world that was spiraling out of control. I needed to let that version of myself go in order to embrace the best version of my truest self.

Once I had stripped the weight of all expectations and fully accepted the new version of me, all the pieces began to fall into place. Unexpectedly, I was offered the opportunity to take an early retirement. It was truly a gift from God as I was only thirty-one at that time and this had never before been offered by the company. It was my freedom. Suddenly I was facing the chance for a new life and a clean slate. I was always someone who sided with security, but this time I was empowered with a whole new self-realization and clear vision. I boldly took the leap. Just as I'd envisioned, this started the beginning of a new phase in my life which led to the discovery of my true calling.

I stepped out as a freelancer and watched my work take off. Then, I decided to take another leap to start my own consulting company. I continued to do more of what I loved with clients I enjoyed. I shaped my vision for what I wanted to create.

At that time, my mom was still seriously ill, so I was the most open-hearted, emotionally raw, introspective, spiritually-in-touch, and purpose-driven that I'd ever been. My guard was down, and my heart was open. I wanted to create a life based on purpose, lived with passion, and filled with prosperity. I wanted to get up every day and do work I loved for people I enjoyed and get paid generously. I had a vision in my mind's eye of the life I wanted to live. This new vision became the foundation for my business and life based on purpose. Twenty years later, I look back and see that everything that manifested over these years did so through this exercise.

While my career was thriving, there were other areas of my life that remained unstable. My mom's health had diminished greatly, so much so, that she remained bedridden for ten years. Even with my family trying to help navigate her MS diagnosis, our resources and help were limited. The burden of my mom's illness rested on my shoulders like a thousand-pound weight. It took over my every thought and occupied my emotions. No matter what I was doing, my mother's illness was always on my mind.

Finally, one night after crying out to God, I released my worries to him. I can't explain the freedom I felt except to say that I could breathe again. Over time, when I started feeling consumed by these feelings again, I would pray to God and let it go. I learned a new way of dealing with these overwhelming emotions, and trusted God to share in my burden.

Not long after releasing this worry to God, a miracle happened. A friend told us about a world-renowned doctor who just happened to practice right in our backyard in Atlanta, Georgia. He specialized in multiple sclerosis and was conducting his most current research at Harvard. We made an appointment. He immediately admitted my mother to the hospital where she began a radical treatment. Her care continued monthly for over a year. Then it happened. Our miracle. My mom *walked*! The doctor said he had never seen anything like this before. After ten years of being bedridden, my mom was free. She was given a second chance at life. We were blessed with having our mom back. I cannot express the joy this brought to our lives, and the life it brought back to my family. I began to feel real joy again.

My life had changed so much over those ten years from the vulnerable woman who was isolated and alone in her new town. I was now empowered by my choices and my clarity. I experienced the fullness of the rewards that came from following the path offered to me. I was living my manifested life, except for one part: my marriage. There was only one thing left to do.

I believe our hero's journey will continue until we take our last breath. The clocks on the wall are a daily reminder that time moves quickly. There's no reason to keep waiting and guessing if you're on the right path. Honor yourself and look at your past, or how I like to refer to it is, revisit your hero's journey. Finally, make sense of what seems like a mess, and then create a path to your purpose. *Begin each day as if you had wings, follow your dreams, and say yes to a beautiful life.*

# PATH TO YOUR POWER

## YOUR HERO'S JOURNEY

I believe we all have our own different choices that help strengthen and develop us. If you find yourself lost, or at a major transition in your life, the pathway offered below can be the beginning of the end to your day-to-day suffering.

Start with the end. Most people want to start at the beginning. What I mean is *end the suffering* first. To do this, you must revisit your past, which I call our Hero's Journey. Embrace the pain, make sense of the mess, collect the gems, and know that it's divinely guided to serve and strengthen you for your higher purpose.

Be willing to create a pathway to your purpose. Pivot just enough so that you are able to start to understand what you're here to teach and whom you're meant to serve. It's okay if this takes some time. The most important step is being willing for it to be something completely different than you are thinking right now.

Begin your new life. Buy a notebook. It doesn't have to be fancy; what's important is you make time daily to reconcile your past. Start to understand the past choices you made and forgive yourself and others. Then, think about your future. Write out what you want it to feel and look like. Don't think about how, when, where, who — any of it. Just write your dream life on paper. In other words, vision cast your life.

## ABOUT

Jennifer Bridges is a business and life coach helping others get to their next level *on purpose*. She's passionate about inspiring, influencing, and impacting the journey and success of women. She is dedicated to helping them discover their purpose, create their vision, align their natural gifts, and take their big leap. Jennifer is most passionate about the three-step process she's developed in your Hero's Journey that helps you reach your BIG dream. She offers both individual sessions and breakthrough retreat experiences. Her clients are blown away by Jennifer's uncanny ability to tap into their purpose and help build their path to future prosperity. Find out more at JenniferBridges.com.

When Jennifer isn't working, which is rare, you can find her tooling around Athens, Alabama, or spending cherished time with friends in Atlanta, Georgia — Jennifer's second home. She also loves the outdoors, nature, and her two grown nieces. Jennifer is also a former basketball player and has been known to still throw the occasional three-pointer.

# A NOTE FROM ALLYSON

Here's where I introduce you to Misty. Why the special introduction? Because of all the authors featured in this anthology, I've worked with her the longest. I met Misty at a time when her son was just learning to walk, her career was struggling to move forward, and Misty felt stuck. She also believed that the solutions to her problems were "out there somewhere," and that she needed to bring them to her. She was overwhelmed, exhausted, and emotional.

Through our work together, Misty was having one major revelation after another, so much so, that her world seemed to be turning upside down. When she realized that she was having a breakthrough, she calmed down and fully embraced the work with a determination and fierceness I hadn't before seen. With her eye on the prize, Misty healed the remaining wounds that kept getting in her way and made a life-changing decision to have it all! "Why limit myself?" was a question that forever altered her life.

By applying everything she's learned through working with me and being committed to her daily practice of Personalized Science, Misty finally has everything she wants, and if you talk to her, she will excitedly share that she's nowhere near finished. Here's her story of becoming the woman who has everything she wants — and how YOU can join her on that journey.

# NOTES AND REFLECTIONS

# CHAPTER 7

# MY JOURNEY TO BECOMING . . . BY MISTY BLAKESLEY

*Integrating the spiritual into the physical manifests tangible results including meaningful relationships, dream homes, fulfilling careers or callings, money in the bank, and so much more.*

My face is soaked with tears. It's cold outside but I am sweating. I am stuck in this car, riding four-and-a-half hours to North Carolina to see my sister, nieces, and mom. Three hours in and I have been sobbing the entire time. I mean ugly crying, the kind of crying where your entire body is shaking, your nose is running, and your face is contorted. I have another hour-and-a-half left to my trip and there is no end in sight to these tears. My heart is broken; it is shattered, and I don't know how to fix it.

It's been three months. Three months since my world was turned upside down. This isn't like me. I always "fix" things. I fix my things, and come to think of it, I fix everyone else's things, too. I am a "pick yourself up, fix your makeup, and power through" kind of girl. Why is it so hard this time? Why are my methods not working?

You see, three months ago, I lost the promise of my little girl, my Sara Jane. With devastating news, my pregnancy ended at sixteen weeks, and my husband and I lost our little girl and the promise of what we believed that meant for us. Pink bows and ballet. Lots of frilly clothes and a daddy's girl. We were both grieving for what we had lost and the way we had lost it.

I allow myself a couple of weeks to process and accept what has happened and then it is back to work. I hide my pain. I don't want anyone to know how bad it still hurts. I will dry my eyes and pull it together, so my family won't see. So that no one sees, not even my husband.

The trip home from North Carolina was just the same–four-and-a-half hours of intense emotion and heart wrenching, soul crushing sobs. It was during that drive, however, that my life would change forever. It was in those moments that I realized that I needed help, that I was not going to find my way through this alone. It was in this moment and from this situation, that I would start my journey to healing. A type of healing and a level of healing I never knew was possible. It would be the start of something amazing, even though there was no way I could see it in those moments.

Once I had complete awareness that I wasn't going to make it through this trauma without help, I set the intention that I would get help. I had no idea who or where. What I did know was that I wasn't interested in clinical therapy. I had been down that path earlier in my life, and it left me more confused and frustrated than when I started. And, more importantly, I knew what I did want: soul level, life-changing healing.

The most wonderful thing about the universe is that when you set an intention with as much emotion and conviction as I had that day, it has no choice but to answer. All that is required of us is to keep an open mind and receive inspired action.

It had been a couple of weeks since that trip to North Carolina. My husband and I were spending time with our closest friends, friends who knew what we had been through. And interestingly enough, they were friends who all wanted to have children and struggled with fertility issues of their own.

As the girls were all huddled around the kitchen, sharing good food, better wine, and wonderful conversation, one of my girlfriends asked me if I had ever heard of Reiki. Reiki? No, I had no idea what this was! She proceeded to enlighten me. I was fascinated by all that she was saying. The next day, I did what most do: I Googled it. That search led me to my first healer. She is a Reiki, EFT, and Energy Healer. The moment I saw her website, I knew this was for me. I scheduled my consultation and, soon after, began this very new and exciting journey.

Like many, my goals include healthy relationships, love, the gift of children, a successful career or calling that fills me with purpose, and wealth! Yes, I crave abundance, prosperity, health, and wealth. I wanted it all, and all at the same time. I choose not one or the other but everything simultaneously (spoiler alert: yes, you can have it all!).

Acquiring knowledge of energy and spiritual healing isn't just for healers or those wanting to become healers. This work is for everyone! This knowledge will send you down a path to creating the life you've always desired. I use all of my knowledge to create tangible and physical success in my personal and professional life.

For me and my work, it is important that others recognize that spiritual knowledge isn't separate from worldly knowledge. And spiritual work isn't separate from worldly work. The key is integrating the spiritual into the physical, manifesting real and tangible results like meaningful relationships, children, your dream house, a fulfilling career or calling, immense amounts of money in your bank account, and more!

**If you are brand new to this journey, or have been on this road for some time, there are three profound lessons that I wish to share:**

- First, this journey is yours alone.
- Second, setting strong boundaries is critical for your healing and growth.
- Third, money work is never about the money.

When I first discovered all that is energy healing, I was blown away. And, like most people, when we stumble upon profound, life-changing knowledge, we want to share it with everyone we love and care about. We begin telling our partners, spouses, siblings, and closest friends. And as we experience life change after life change, tangible result after result, our desire to bring those closest to us along increases exponentially.

For me, the person I most desired to bring along was my husband. I thought, *If I can create these kinds of results by myself, imagine what we could achieve if we did this together!* I know many of you are like, *YES! That is my thought exactly.* And like many of you, I tried and tried to "encourage" him to join in. To say he was not interested in the least is an understatement.

My ongoing effort led to a lot of frustration and tension for me and the person I love the most. I am grateful that he has what seems to be never-ending patience for me. In this experience, my husband was the teacher. He taught me that it is possible to share an incredible bond, love, and life, while experiencing very separate journeys. He has always given me space to explore every aspect of myself, all the while showing me and my experiences the highest level of support and respect. And I found that when I provided him that same space, support, and respect, my room to explore grew, as did his.

The lesson here: **this journey is your own.** You cannot bring anyone with you. And the harder your try, the slower your progress becomes. This particular journey doesn't work this way. It's not like sharing a dream vacation or enjoying a five-star meal. And for this, I am most grateful, as this is the most personal journey you will ever take, diving into your closest held secrets, your deepest (and sometimes insidious) guilt and shame, and all those beliefs that hold you hostage.

What I now realize is that we all manifest wonderful and amazing experiences and material possessions in the most unique and personal way. My husband is a master manifester. He may not call it that. But he does create the life he wants, in the way that feels most natural to him.

When we allow everyone in our lives to grow, expand, love, and experience in their own time and in their own way, we begin to experience a beautiful unity, peace, and calm within. I encourage you to follow your inspiration when it comes to how and with whom you share your journey. You may choose to share information or keep it sacred. And do all of this knowing that the universe is always supporting you and your loved ones. The universe has a way of delivering all you desire without the direct participation of your loved ones. The universe continues to deliver to me over and over without requiring joint participation from my loved ones, even my husband.

Once I understood that this was my journey alone, I began to understand that I am like a turtle, making my way to the vast sea where anything is possible, and where I can be, do, and have anything. And the quickest way to do that was to unload all those I had tried to carry on my back and take with me, to allow them to find their own way to the sea, knowing that we would all end up there eventually.

This is where things get interesting. You see, many knew me as the turtle. For thirty-five-plus years, they knew me this way. I played a role in their lives, a role they had come to depend on and that I had become quite comfortable with (although, not happy about). For some, I was a mediator. Some, a door mat. Others, a pushover. Don't misunderstand, not everyone in my life treated me in one of these ways. And I have my husband and a couple of very close friends that have always loved me in a very healthy way and have watched me morph into a very independent, boundary-rich individual. It has been a very rewarding journey for me, and I enjoy the validation they provide when they express the ways they have seen me change, expand, and grow.

**Setting boundaries** in places where none have existed can be hard and trying. That being said, it is critical. And it is really important that you understand, boundaries are all about YOU, not others. This has been a decade-long journey for me. And the toughest place to build boundaries for me was within my family.

I grew up with two sisters and both my parents until age thirteen, when my father passed away from cancer. We all played a role in this family unit, and these roles morphed and then amplified after the loss of my father. And these roles served us in some way at the time. That is the conundrum: since they served us then, most of us tend to take these familial roles with us into adulthood, where they very rarely continue to serve us. It is why so many of us dread holidays and other events that bring us all back together again, under one roof. For me, I continued to serve as the compliant mediator within my family. I was the one that placated everyone to keep peace. I was known as the peace maker. That role in and of itself isn't bad, until you compromise all of your personal desire for the "good of the group," to the point where you are no longer happy or enjoying yourself.

As I began to become the strong, independent, successful women I knew I could be, I began to implement boundaries. Doing this requires all those in my life to observe and respect the woman that I am now and that I continue to become. It requires those who have known me since birth to see me with a new lens. That this is as much a journey for them as it has been for me. What I have learned is how to hold space full of love for those people, as they adjust to my new expectations for how I am to be treated and supported.

For anyone experiencing this now or maybe realizing this is a must next step, please remember to have grace for yourself and your loved ones. This journey tends to be a transition that happens over time, one boundary at a time. You will get there and so will your loved ones. The space between can be filled with times of non-communication, feel like a hiatus, or simply feel a bit distant. Just know that the boundaries you set are absolutely worth it. You are worth it. And remember, the universe is always here to support us on our journey to self-love, enlightenment, and expansion. Especially when we do so from a place of absolute love.

The last message I wish to impart is about money. Why money? Because, in this humanly experience, on this planet, money is the energetically neutral (paper and naturally occurring metals) used to provide material goods (home, food, heat, electricity) and, most of all, FREEDOM. Another reason I believe this message is important is because it's the reason I hear most often for not investing in personal healing. When I started this journey, I wanted healing and a baby. And I got both, fast. And once I had him, I started to see the other areas in my life where I wanted more. More time, more money, more freedom. I wanted to be the best wife and mother I could be without sacrificing a career that also brought me fulfillment and joy. Having it all with complete balance seemed elusive at first. And, like my previous experience, once I began to focus my awareness and healing around this desire, the universe delivered. In spades!

If you take nothing else away from the words I share with you in this text, please remember this, **your money story has nothing to do with money itself**. Let me say that again, YOUR MONEY STORY HAS NOTHING TO DO WITH MONEY ITSELF. Whether you are elbow deep in lack or standing on a wave of wealth you wish to take higher, your current money story is completely tied to your current belief system. And it's not just tied to your belief system about money; it is tied to your belief system about YOU.

To make this even clearer, most of us start our healing journey by dropping a belief system that isn't even our own, but the system that was handed down to us by our parents, family, and church. And that belief system has been passed down from generation to generation. Most of us are holding onto belief systems that no longer serve us, simply because of the strength and depth of our commitment to the known and the paralyzing fear of the unknown. It's our fear of what might happen if we let go of all we know for the opportunity to explore many things we do not. Your fear is trying to protect you from getting hurt, but in reality, it is holding you hostage to the very things you are trying to escape.

My profound and confident belief in this truth is based on my own personal experiences. Letting go of the known to pursue the unknown is scary! And it is worth it! I encourage you to show yourself grace. And to do so, while you take a leap of faith, and jump into a journey that will forever change you and your reality for the better.

There were many times I invested in healing and coaching for myself, not knowing how all the money would come together. I have made that investment through credit cards and payment plans. Why did I invest? Because I craved the life of abundance. Deep down, I knew life didn't have to be hard. I could see it in examples all around me. I knew many that made six-figure incomes working less than thirty-two hours a week. And I knew if they could achieve that, then so could I. I just didn't know how. So, I hired a teacher, a life coach, and a spiritual mentor. Almost a decade later, after experiencing exponential growth that led to expanding my money multiple times, I still invest in this. Why? Because denial is strong. If we are the only thing standing between the life we have now and the life we truly desire, then there are some hard truths hiding inside. It is impossible to see our blind spots without help. And why is it so important to have someone or something that can see our blind spots? Because it can CHANGE and even SAVE our lives.

So, this memoir is dedicated to my Sara Jane. Thank you for setting me on a journey only sixteen weeks (of pregnancy) with you could have started. Thank you for blessing my life in ways I never knew would be possible even though you are on the other side. Thank you, my sweet baby girl, for all you inspire in me. And thank you for sending me Liam, the rainbow baby you knew my heart needed.

I no longer believe in coincidence. I believe all things are orchestrated based on our desires. And if you desire a new, abundant life, filled with all good things, then I believe that is why you are reading my words. If my journey is inspiring you, then take your inspired action, NOW! Don't wait; the life you crave is right in front of you. Invite a teacher into your life that can show you how to step into your love, abundance, prosperity, health, and wealth!

## ABOUT

Misty Blakesley, MBA, is an Executive Leader and trained Healer who teaches the importance of integrating your spiritual practice and personal magic into the real world so that you can restore your birthright to love, abundance, prosperity, and wealth.

Misty's professional training includes a twenty-year-plus year career in sales, sales training, and sales leadership. She serves as an executive leader in the tech space. She is also trained as a Master Reiki Energy Healer, Ancient Symbology Energy Healer, and is studying to become a RTT (Rapid Transformational Therapy) Therapist.

You can find and connect with Misty at linkedin.com/in/MistyBlakesley.

# A SPECIAL GIFT FROM ALLYSON

As you're reading this amazing book, you're beginning to more clearly understand that you are not alone, no matter what you are facing right now. Through the moving stories inside these pages, you are discovering that there is hope, and that it's possible to accomplish the goals to make your dreams come true.

But let's face it, life can be challenging. This is especially true when you don't understand what's happening inside (or outside) of you. You do all the right things. You are "a good person." You're responsible, caring, loving, compassionate, generous, kind . . . and yet, you somehow always end up right back where you started — no matter what you try to change to create a different reality.

It's not you . . . it's your brain. It's the truth.

Your brain has a part of it called "the reptilian" and its job is to keep you safe, to keep you the same. Yet to make changes in your life and get different results than what you've had so far, you have to do things differently.

That doesn't mean go out and try many different things (or the same thing) over and over because that only yields more frustration, and you won't be any further ahead. In fact you'll likely move backwards.

To help you begin creating the right foundation for making the changes you want to make, I have prepared a special gift just for you: *Becoming the Boss of Your Brain!* This gift will help you slow down, acknowledge your feelings and emotions, and honor who you are. You've made it through all of life's challenges you've faced so far, and you **can** create a different life than the one you have right now.

Just go to AllysonRoberts.com/gift and tell us where to send it.

Thanks for letting all of us be part of your journey!

**Allyson**

# NOTES AND REFLECTIONS

# CHAPTER 8

# THE SPIRAL STAIRCASE BY KIM NISHIDA

*Claiming our power or giving it away is a choice we make. Tackling unworthiness was the turning point in creating a better life for online marketing strategist turned intuitive energy worker and passionate animal and human rights activist.*

I'm clutching an oversized, faded, and slightly ratty sweatshirt as close to my body as I can, just to keep the wind from cutting right through me; I can't stop shivering. This is a summer day at Ocean Beach on the westside of San Francisco. Although the waves are still sparkling, the fog has already begun rolling back towards the city and the sun has retreated for the day. Sand has crept uncomfortably into my sneakers and socks, and I feel like a nerd, but it's much too cold to walk barefoot.

This is the day I'm hoping to win my boyfriend back. I'm 20 years old. Even though we broke up more than a year ago, I'm still following him and his friends around like a stray dog begging for attention.

He had called me up to ask if I wanted to hang out at the beach, and of course, I thought he'd meant just the two of us. So when he honked his horn to pick me up, I was disappointed to see that I would have to cram into the back seat with three other girls who seemed to have zero interest in talking to me.

Still, it had been a fun day. We played beach volleyball, drank wine coolers, and ate hot dogs with soggy buns and too much mustard. We walked for miles and miles until the fog rolled in.

And then it happened . . .

My ex-boyfriend slows down to let the others get ahead and pulls me aside. My heart leaps as he edges closer to me. Surely this is the moment when he admits we should never have broken up. That he's been an ass and can't imagine living his life without me. My heart is beating so hard, I wonder if he can hear it.

He leans so close I can smell his familiar smell, then points to one of the other girls and whispers, "Do you think she'll say yes if I ask her out? I've had a huge crush on her for a while. I can't believe how smart she is. And funny!"

He's doing it in a friendly way, because after all, we're supposed to be just friends. But I can't breathe, and I wonder how I'm still conscious. For the next few minutes all I can do is watch him flirting with her in ways that used to make my heart race and my body melt. I know I should just ignore them, but I can't tear my eyes away.

When the agony of watching the two of them flirt in that "new love" sort of way is finally over and we walk back to his beat up 1950s Chevy Bel Air, he turns back to me and says, "Hey, give me the keys!" Suddenly, I remember he gave me the job of holding the car keys because I'm the "dependable friend."

I snap to attention, saying, "Of course!" and reach into the kangaroo pocket of my sweatshirt. But instead of keys, I'm only grasping air. I don't think my heart could drop any further or simultaneously beat any faster. For the next hour, as the temperature plummets and the skies darken, I endure the glares of my ex, his new flirt, and the rest of his friends as we comb the beach searching in vain. Finally, just after twilight, he smashes the passenger window to unlock his car so we can hotwire the ignition and drive silently home.

One more thing . . . during the sixty odd minutes of desperately searching for those car keys, I snuck behind the public restrooms, stuck my finger down my throat as I had done countless times before, and made myself throw up. And for a second or two, I felt a tiny bit better.

In that moment, as I hid behind that dirty, putrid, cinderblock outhouse, I had the crystal-clear realization that I was using bulimia to punish myself. Yes, I lost the keys. I screwed up. My boyfriend doesn't love me. Girls are shooting daggers at me with their eyes. I feel like a complete loser. Unlovable. Unworthy. And the only thing that makes me feel better is punishing myself.

But that doesn't mean I deserve to be punished. I made a mistake, but that doesn't make me a mistake.

Just like that, it was over. That was the last time I ever purged.

In that moment, I decided to take my power back, to turn around from the descending path I'd been winding down for so many years and to start climbing up, back towards the light of the truth of who I am.

This sudden shift happened after years of bulimia. Years of lying and telling myself that I loved to eat but didn't want to get fat. Years of hiding my habits from my friends and family because I thought they wouldn't understand. Years of feeling ashamed on Thanksgiving Day and any other holiday after I had just stuffed my face and then purged when no one was around.

At the time, I didn't understand that all of this came about because I was so busy tap-dancing through life. Trying to entertain others, get people to love me or at least like me, even if that meant pretending to be someone I wasn't.

For decades, I had given my power away because of fear. Fear of failure, of people finding out I was a fraud. Fear of being an outcast.

Before that day on the beach, I didn't realize how much my choices were affecting my happiness. I allowed my dreams to be crushed because I believed I wasn't worthy.

Here's an example: I wanted to be a writer since I was old enough to hold a pencil. I wrote stories and poetry day and night and dreamed of being a celebrated novelist. I had a closet full of notebooks filled with stories stacked almost as tall as I was.

And then one day a high school math teacher told me, "Writers don't make money. Being a writer isn't responsible or realistic."

So instead of pursuing a creative writing degree, I gave up on my dream and majored in civil engineering. It's weird because my parents never encouraged me to give up writing and become an engineer. But somehow I got it into my head that this is what was best for me and what would make them happy.

This one assumption triggered a failure of epic proportions.

First of all, because I focused mainly on writing and the arts in high school, suddenly declaring myself to be a civil engineering major was a red flag on my college applications.

I was rejected by every single school I applied to, except for one: the university just a stone's throw away from where I lived with my parents. This was a crushing defeat for me. Although I loved my family, I was bursting to leave the nest and spread my wings. Going to school less than three miles from home meant I'd be staying put.

One night, sitting on my twin bed with the yellow canopy top, I stared at the brand-new set of luggage my parents had surprised me with when they thought I would be leaving for college soon. I sobbed, utterly heartbroken.

Back in those days, there was an appeal system in place at the university I had fallen in love with in Berkeley. I filled out a new application, convinced teachers to write me letters of recommendation, painstakingly crafted my appeal letter, sent in the packet, and prayed.

A few months later, my prayers were answered when a "fat" envelope arrived with a gold sticker on it that said, "Welcome to the Class of 1988." When I tore into that envelope, I cried tears of joy, but also relief. I was on my way to becoming a civil engineer and, in turn, a responsible member of society. Say goodbye to my silly dreams of being a writer.

I packed my suitcases and was on my way to college. But there was still this problem of being a closeted novelist trapped in the body of a budding civil engineer. I actually had no clue what civil engineers even did. And, it turns out, my aptitude and natural talent for it were next to nothing.

I went from being a published young poet who graduated third in my class, to receiving another letter from the university informing me that my grades were so dismal, I was on academic probation. I had just one semester to pull my grades up or I would get kicked out of school. Because I was used to easily earning A's, the sudden nosedive into a C-average was mortifying. I began binge-eating to cope with the stress.

I felt in my bones that I was a fraud, but I desperately tried to convince those around me that I had my act together.

Unfortunately, I tied my grades to my self-worth, and I quickly developed that eating disorder in an effort to feel like I was in control. Binging and purging became a daily habit in those college days before I decided enough was enough that day on the beach.

Even though I was smart enough to quickly transfer out of civil engineering and into English literature and start earning A's instead of C's and D's, the damage was done. My self-esteem was shot and deteriorated into self-destructive behavior. This included allowing myself to get into emotionally abusive relationships both in my personal and working life, all because I was trying to be someone I'm not.

I convinced myself that I was never meant to be a writer. I honestly didn't know who I was anymore because I looked to others to validate my thoughts and feelings.

I wanted my family to be proud of me (and they were). I wanted people to like me (and they did). I wanted to be "successful." But somehow, I also felt like if I made one wrong move, everyone would turn their backs on me and I'd be out on the street, unloved and fated to die alone.

I felt like I was descending a narrow spiral staircase taking me away from the real me. Each step wound me around to a place that felt both familiar and a little bit further away from who I yearned to be. In fact, I had wandered so far down the rabbit hole that I couldn't even see daylight anymore.

That's how I gave my power away, one step at a time.

I was telling myself it was okay to compromise, to give up on my dreams, to do what others told me to do in order to fit in, to feel ashamed of who I was or to accept I was broken. I was convinced I had to work hard in order to "earn my keep" in the world. I believed that following my own dreams was selfish.

Each thought that I wasn't good enough was one more step down that spiral staircase leading me to that rock bottom, yet empowering, moment at the beach.

My life got a bit better after that. I stopped chasing the ex-boyfriend. I landed a great job in book publishing in San Francisco. I made new friends.

But climbing up the spiral staircase was much harder than climbing down! It felt like an ascent of Everest proportions. Take one step, stop, try to breathe, take another step. Each step forward was punctuated by my mind screaming, *Give up. It's too late. You're not worthy. What in the world do you think you're doing? It's not safe to go in this direction. No one gave you permission to turn around!*

Even though those thoughts shook and terrified me, I kept moving forward. Take one step, stop, breathe. Take another step. Baby steps.

Because this ascent was a spiral instead of a straight line, I would often feel like I was right back where I started. But when I took the time to think about it, I realized that maybe I was just a little bit higher in life than I was before. A little less hard on myself. A little less fearful.

Along my journey, I continued to fool myself and everyone around me. I can share countless stories of how I portrayed myself as confident when I was anything but. When I started my own business, I convinced other entrepreneurs and business leaders that I was outgoing and extroverted, when I'm actually super shy and definitely an introvert. I remember dressing up and attending parties or networking events and having the worst stomach cramps from stress as I put a smile on my face to hide the pain.

There were moments when I had glimpses of my true self. I would gain confidence in who I thought I was and even become quite successful in my career. I did this several times. But each time I would find a way to sabotage myself. I'd lose interest in what I was doing and I'd either quit my job or make really poor decisions that landed me in the wrong place at the wrong time.

I attracted the worst clients and let them walk all over me. And then I would stop, breathe, and take another step. I'd say goodbye to situations with toxic clients, and over time, found clients who treated me with respect and deep appreciation.

Today I get paid really well for my writing. I'm married to the love of my life who sees the real me and loves me for it. I had the courage to turn away from really lucrative work in order to explore my intuitive side and nurture my dreams of being an energy worker and animal communicator.

There are extraordinary moments each day when I consciously choose to follow my heart, to open up and trust my intuition. I see the glorious light of who I am and who I'm truly meant to be. I'm no longer trying to please others by being anything other than myself.

I'm a work in progress for sure, and I'm not at the top of that staircase yet. I have good days and bad days and that's okay. I'm thoroughly enjoying the journey; and I can look back at the "bad" times and feel immense gratitude for where I've been and where I'm going.

# PATH TO YOUR POWER

## THE STEPS TO STOP HIDING

When I was asked to be a co-author in this anthology, I took a deep look within to find the nuggets I thought would help you the most. Below are a few things that made a big difference for me along the way. My wish is that they provide you with insight and courage to finally shine!

When you work hard to please others, you might be hiding your true self. Trying to please others is an unconscious survival mechanism. You're not sure exactly when it happens. My deepest encouragement is for you to make the decision that Enough is Enough! When I decided that I'd had enough, I was over it. I was over caring about what others thought about me. I was over trying to get others to like me by being someone I'm not. You are enough!

Start somewhere . . . anywhere. When we are in the thick of it all, it may seem overwhelming to think about big changes. The thing is, every small step gets us there. For me, I needed some self-assurance. I remind myself: I am safe; I have permission to be myself; I am worthy; I am enough, and I'm never alone.

Reclaim your choices. Every day we have two choices. The first is to claim our power and the second is to give it away. While it may not *feel* a choice at first, the realization of this changed my life forever.

Be willing to ask yourself some hard questions. Over time, I learned that when I stop and ask myself three crucial questions, I'm able to reclaim parts of myself that I might be giving away unconsciously. The first is, "Who am I when I'm standing in my power?" The second is, "How do I feel when I know I'm not standing in it?" and lastly,

"How do I want to feel today?" Asking and answering these questions can change your entire day.

You have the power within to change your story. Whatever we believe about ourselves is true. It doesn't matter what anyone else believes. You can think, *I'm worthless* or *I'm a gift to myself and others*. How you feel as well as your reality will be based on whichever thought you believe. While it isn't always easy, each new day brings us the opportunity to look at our thoughts and direct them up instead of down. *That* is powerful!

## ABOUT

Kim Nishida is an avid writer and all-around book geek and an online marketing strategist turned intuitive energy worker. A graduate from UC Berkeley in English literature, she practices animal communication, writes poetry, and creates inspirational artwork in her spare time. Although, as an entrepreneur, she has spent decades helping clients with business and marketing, she's now following her heart and divine guidance to assist other "dear hearts and beautiful souls" activate their own intuitive powers and align with their true purpose. Find out more about Kim and request free downloadable resources to help you connect your head with your heart and soul at www.Kim-Nishida.com/intuitive-arts/

During her personal time, Kim can be found at her desk writing, reading, and creating fun things. She also just happens to be a passionate animal and human rights activist.

# NOTES AND REFLECTIONS

## CHAPTER 9

# UNBROKEN BY LINDA MOYNIHAN-WEIKEL

*The path to recovery, healing, and loving yourself is a circuitous process that can include freeing a part of you that's been buried for years. It also leads to methods of healing that are unexpected, yet effective.*

Who would have ever thought that at sixty-four years of age I would be talking to my deceased ex-husband in an empty chair? How did I end up here? While others may think that this is crazy nonsense, this crazy nonsense has come after a long lifetime journey of self-discovery, self-love, and changing mindset. Did this journey help me to become the person that I want to be or was this journey finding the person that I had always been, but was buried in self-doubt?

At twenty-one, having just graduated from college, I met the man that I was destined to marry. We met in the summer of 1978, while, of all things, operating a roller coaster ride together for an amusement park. I think this was the first sign of many to come from the Universe. Warning! Be aware this relationship is destined to have many ups and downs.

Dave and I hit it off right away. He was easy to talk to; we had the same interests and we loved to laugh together. He was also very cute. We started dating a few days later. From the moment we met, we spent all of our free time together going to movies, baseball games, sailing the San Francisco Bay, snow skiing–you name it, we did it together. We enjoyed each other's company, and we married the following May, in 1979. I *thought* I could be my true self in this relationship.

However, once we became engaged and were planning our wedding, our differences in upbringing became more and more apparent. I grew up in the same home from the age of three, until I married Dave at twenty-two. My parents were happily married. We would eat our meals together, take family vacations, go camping, snow skiing, and travel all over the United States, Mexico, and Canada. My parents supported any activities and clubs that my sisters or I participated in and would attend all of our functions. We talked, argued, and loved each other. I lived in a neighborhood where we all came together to celebrate holidays, birthdays, and have the occasional block party.

Dave's family consisted of his father, stepmother, and three siblings. His parents had moved quite a bit during Dave's childhood. When we met, he had been estranged from his birth mother, and his family had lost communication with his younger brother. His parents were cold and distant, not what you would call a warm and fuzzy family. There was little communication and/or parental support; it was a family that was just going through the motions. I would later learn that Dave also grew up in a family of verbal and physical abuse, created by his father.

Years later, after having two daughters of our own, I would often tell them that when you fall in love and want to marry, look behind the man, as his family and all of their baggage comes with him. A marriage is not just a man and woman, but a whole familial tribe.

Prior to our marriage, Dave and I did not discuss how we would budget money, the number of children we wanted, goals for the future, where we wanted to live, etc. We also did not discuss our deepest darkest fears, desires, and wishes. I married Dave from emotion and love, not knowing the true man.

After the wedding, his controlling side began to slowly appear. He had read the book, *Dress for Success* and wanted me to follow it. He wanted me to wear suits instead of the dresses I loved. He would criticize the clothes that I chose to wear to social events and even criticized my jeans that had flaps on the pockets. He would tell me that the jean pockets made my butt look big. At the time, I was 5'6" and 120 pounds. Words are powerful! To this day, I hear him whispering in my ear, "Do not wear jeans with that design."

My dream was to have a partnership, dividing house chores, paying bills, etc. Dave's response was that the men in his family do not do dishes. Therefore, I quickly learned that I was in charge of the daily household chores. Major purchases were not discussed. He wanted the latest electronics, and so purchased entire stereo systems and even a car, all without discussing it with me or reviewing our budget! Our credit card debt began to rise. Since Dave did not want to be bothered with the bills, I took over the budgeting, balancing of the checkbook, and dealt with the anxiety of where I was going to find the money to pay our bills. I slowly began to realize that this marriage was not a partnership.

Over the years, I noticed that he began demonstrating a Dr. Jekyll and Mr. Hyde personality. One minute happy-go-lucky, then something would trigger him, and he would explode with verbal and emotional abuse. My daughters and I felt like we were walking on eggshells most of the time. At times, I would stand up for myself; other times I would take flight and leave home for a few hours. I became a pro at being passive aggressive. In the early years of our marriage, Dave would also take flight. We began a pattern that continued throughout our marriage.

We were young; he was twenty-two years old when we married, too. I had graduated from college a year earlier and Dave had dropped out of college after two years. Hindsight is always 20/20. Dave had not been able to experience a life beyond his toxic family life. I, on the other hand, had not lived on my own or supported myself independently. I would not experience that part of life until in my mid-forties, after our divorce.

On the outside I appeared strong, outgoing, secure, and happy in my own skin. In reality, I was full of anxiety, and in an unhappy marriage. I allowed others to influence me in every part of my life. I became the peacekeeper, always trying to make everyone happy, never wanting anyone to be mad at me. I was trained at an early age by my parents to accept my responsibility for being involved in another's bad actions. Now, it was always my fault no matter what. I slowly began to lose myself, forgetting what I wanted and needed. I never established boundaries or demanded how I wanted to be treated. I was slowly morphing into the person that I thought everyone wanted me to be, therefore slowly losing the person that I was born to be.

In my thirties, I slowly began to try to find my voice, but this soon became a high price to pay for myself, and my daughters. For years, I had begged Dave to make the girls' breakfast, so that I could get ready for work, as his employer offered flextime, while mine did not. Dave refused. He was not a morning person and did not want to get out of bed early. One particular morning, I found my youngest crawling on top of the counter trying to get a bowl down for cereal. I came into our bedroom, furious, yelling: why couldn't he get out of bed and help me? Dave lunged out of bed, pushed me against the wall, and put his hand around my throat. He then proceeded to tell me that I was never to speak to him that way again.

Shame and guilt rose high that day. How could I have chosen this man to be the father of my children? Unfortunately, my oldest daughter witnessed her father with his hand around my throat. Years later, she confessed from that traumatic day on, she would flinch when her dad tried touching her, even out of love. She also confessed that she hates anyone touching her neck. So being the passive aggressive person that I was, I went into silent mode. I got the girls ready for school and myself ready for work.

I was a special education teacher and went to work acting like it was just a normal day, never revealing that my husband had just physically attacked me. That day, I vowed to myself that I would never again ask Dave for help getting our daughters ready. That night, Dave and I discussed what had happened.

I told him that I did not want to end up like his stepmother who had been physically abused by his father throughout their marriage. I wanted us to go to counseling, but unfortunately that never happened. I continued to stay in this toxic marriage, thinking it was best for our daughters and me. I kept telling myself that if I could change my mindset, things would get better.

I began to read self-help books: *Men are From Mars and Women are from Venus*, by John Gray, and *Divorce Busting* by Michele Weiner-Davis. Both of these books helped immensely at the time, but it was not sustainable. I kept assuming that things would change. I was always thinking that Dave could read my mind and I believed that he, in turn, thought I could read his mind to cater to his needs. Once again, I was trying to change myself to save our marriage. Dave, on the other hand, was not. I was giving 110%, filling his emotional pot while mine continued to stay empty.

In 1993, Dave was offered a position in Atlanta, Georgia, and we decided to move our family across country. I was leaving behind a strong support system consisting of family, friends, and a job that I loved. Once we arrived, Dave stopped being intimate with me. He hinted that there was someone else. He started putting up a brick wall.

Once again, I tried to change myself, thinking that I alone could strengthen our marriage. At the time, his employer offered six counseling sessions to all employees and family members. I found a therapist and started going to counseling. I would beg Dave to go with me, so I could improve myself and our relationship, but he refused.

Knowing that there was another woman that Dave was seeing, I decided to also go to the County Health Department for an HIV test. This was definitely a low point in my life. It was an experience I never expected to have and never wanted to have again. I gave Dave a pamphlet when I got home and suggested he take the test; he was furious that I would even suggest it.

He slowly began to withdraw from the family, finding hobbies that would take him away from family time. He started playing his guitar at restaurants or friends' parties, taking flying lessons, scuba diving, and taking vacations by himself or with his friends, never asking me if I would like to join him. Once again, I thought if he was happy, our marriage would be a happy one.

He developed a pattern of putting his friends' needs before the needs of his wife and daughters. He would attend our daughters' dance recitals and their softball games, and even coached my youngest daughter's games. However, if there was a friend in town, or a friend that needed something, he would drop everything for them. Dave's temper began spilling over to our youngest daughter's softball games: yelling at the umpires, etc. This behavior became so bad that coaches did not want our daughter to play on their teams because of his temper.

After Christmas 2001, Dave wrote a letter, addressed it to me, and laid it on the bathroom counter in the middle of the night. It was his way of asking for a divorce. I didn't believe in divorce and no one in my family had been divorced. And if Dave had not asked for a divorce, I would probably still be in a toxic marriage. In September of 2002, our divorce was finalized.

During the divorce process, I didn't want to tell my family or friends, as I was full of shame and guilt; I had a failed marriage. Dave would continually state that it was my fault we were divorcing. This divorce not only affected us, but also our daughters. My oldest daughter, who was away at college, began to have panic attacks. These attacks were so bad that they affected her school performance. I was eventually able to get her into counseling. My youngest was fifteen and she, too, began counseling.

When Dave finally moved out, I realized that I did not miss him. The stress and toxicity of our marriage was gone. The girls and I could relax and not worry about having to walk on eggshells. I began to realize that Dave did me a favor initiating the divorce.

The path to recovery, healing, and loving myself became an eighteen-year baby step process. I enrolled in a "Divorce Recovery" program at our local church. This helped me meet other divorced adults going through the same process of married life to single life. The program focused on children, money, and self-love. This program was just the launching off pad on my journey to recovery.

My healing process has had many ups and downs throughout the years. I started private counseling, but the counselor focused mostly on my childhood and how this was affecting me in my adult life. It did not focus on my mindset and self-love. The healing process consisted of two steps forward and five steps backward as Dave was still in the picture; the father of your children never really goes away.

Even though my girls were adults, they were still adjusting to having divorced parents. A major adjustment was his remarrying, having stepsiblings and a stepmother, and now sharing their father with another family. I also had problems accepting his new marriage. Shame and guilt continued, filling my head with questions. Why weren't the girls and I enough for him? Why was he doing things with his new family that we would beg for him to do with us? I would ask myself, "What's wrong with me? Why am I having difficulty finding someone to date? Why doesn't anyone want to love me?" Dave's off having fun and I am home alone with my cat and dog.

For years, I would continue to hear his voice in my head, telling me that I was a loser, or that something was wrong with me. When I would do home repairs around the house, my anxiety level would begin to rise, and my hands would begin to shake. What if I make a mistake? Someone is going to be mad at me. How could someone continue to have so much hold on me? My daughters were my saviors. They knew what their dad was like, and they would calm me down with comforting words: "Dad's not here," or "If you make a mistake, we can fix it."

I had a repeating dream for many years. In it, there was a body buried in a backyard. I did not know who the person was, but I was always afraid that I would be caught, and the body would be dug up. This dream would mostly occur when I had disagreements with Dave before and after our divorce. At times, I could see the soles of the feet of the body and the last dream I saw the skeleton of the body. After much counseling, I discovered that the body was me. I had buried myself, always trying to be the person everyone wanted me to be, and not the person that I secretly dreamt to be.

With each passing year, I became more accepting of Dave for the person he was and not the person I craved for him to be. In 2018, Dave was diagnosed with pancreatic cancer. All of the baggage that was in our marriage didn't seem to matter anymore. I had to stay strong for our daughters as they watched their father slowly die. In August 2019 the cancer won the battle. It was an extremely difficult time in our lives. My girls and I were struggling, coping with the loss of their father and the unresolved issues they also had with their father.

Five months after Dave's death, the universe directed me to a mindset coach named Allyson Roberts. My youngest daughter and I decided to join a small group facilitated by Allyson. We learned coping skills to deal with our shame and guilt, steps for self-love, and how to deal with our grief.

Even with all of the counseling, books, videos, and divorce recovery programs, I still heard Dave's voice in my head. The words that he spoke to me from twenty-plus years ago would, out of the blue, pop into my head. One night, I just couldn't take it anymore. I was exhausted; why was I continually hearing his voice and the anxiety that accompanied it? Dave had no power over me, he was deceased. Practically in tears, I called Allyson and asked if she had availability for a one-on-one session. I needed his voice out of my head. It had been eighteen years since we divorced. Enough is enough.

This brings me back to the beginning of my story. Why am I talking to my deceased husband in an empty chair? Part of my healing process was finally dealing with my own emotional baggage. I stopped being passive aggressive and trying to bury myself. I visualized Dave in the chair, which he used to sit in when visiting our daughters. I started having the conversations that we never did have during our marriage. I purged my soul. With every conversation that I had, my shame and guilt started to leave my reptilian brain.

With every conversation, my soul is winning and the part of me that was buried is free and can breathe once again.

## PATH TO YOUR POWER

### RESET. REGROUND. RENEW.

If you are facing challenges in your life and feel stuck, please remember that you are not alone. If you are not sure what to do next, know that you don't need to stay in this place. Here are the steps that may help you reset, reground, and find your path forward.

Slow Down. Life is so busy. Before we realize it, we have one hundred things on our list and could easily fit one hundred more. When I notice myself doing this, I know it's to numb the pain. The best advice I can give you is to simply slow down! Ask yourself what rushing around is doing for you, and I promise, you'll see that there's really not much benefit in it at all except to make you feel useful.

Build Relationships. Another area where we have a tendency to rush ourselves is in our relationships with others. Pretend that each relationship is a house. Lay a solid foundation first. Ask a lot of questions. Listen. Don't fill in the blanks. Believe what another person is telling you and base the core of the relationship on real information, and not what you are trying to believe or make the other person into.

Take a Breather. When emotions are high, you have permission to take care of you. Don't meet the irrational demands or expectations of others, especially if your cup is empty. Learn to go for a walk or a drive. Learn to fill up the tub with bubbles and escape. You deserve a time out.

Ask for Help! You are never alone in any given situation — no matter what it is — so find help and receive it. I know we sound like a broken record, BUT in this work we have learned that most of us tread water in our emotional pool until we're almost drowning.

Don't wait until you're panicked, desperate, and freaking out. Ask for help sooner rather than later.

Accept What You Can't Change. Be willing to understand that you cannot control or change anything other than yourself, then do it! Stop waiting for everyone else to "get it together," and finally accept that it isn't going to happen. Later on, if someone does happen to shift, consider it a gift, but it won't matter because you'll be all the better for having changed yourself.

## ABOUT

Linda Moynihan-Weikel is a retired Special Education Teacher who taught for thirty years. She holds a Bachelor of Science degree in Education, a Master of Education with a specialty in Special Education, and a degree of Educational Specialist in Curriculum and Instruction. Linda also earned a National Board teaching certification specializing in Special Education.

In her leisure time, Linda has traveled to all seven continents, volunteered at local schools with her therapy dog, and spends time with her two daughters. She is a native Californian who currently lives in Atlanta, Georgia.

# NOTES AND REFLECTIONS

Shine your light! ♡ Audra Zimpel

## CHAPTER 10

# PERMISSION TO SHINE BY AUDRA ZIMPEL

*Moving from shame, suicidal thoughts, and depression to building a successful career as an intuitive, transformational life/wellness coach. This story of challenge and discovery illustrates the power of perseverance through bouts of clinical depression. You don't need to be perfect to be loved. You are worthy of joy just as you are.*

It's another gorgeous day in LA. The intense light from the blazing California sun blinds me as I walk out of the apartment building. I feel heavy anxiety running through me as I make my way onto the sidewalk. I take jagged breaths trying to keep the tears at bay as I walk to meet my friend, Andy, in the park.

He's concerned about me and doesn't even know how bad off I am. I haven't told him that, for the past three days, I haven't been able to go longer than twenty minutes without sobbing. I've paced my bedroom and cried. My heart has felt like it was going to explode from beating so fast. The shame is consuming me.

Fighting back the tears as I walk down the street, I wonder, *How did I get here? Is this really my life?*

I'm sure everyone driving by on this busy street sees me falling apart. I've let everyone down. I've squandered so many opportunities, both personally and professionally. I can't support myself. I've made so many bad decisions. I've chased a ridiculous acting dream and I've completely failed.

My mind continues racing, *I wanted to make my family proud of me, but all I've done is the opposite. Why couldn't I have chosen a normal career? I'd be married with a mortgage by now. I'm thirty-one years old and I don't have the energy to try again. My strength has left me.*

I see a car speeding down the road toward me. It would be so easy to just walk in front of it. And all the pressure, all the pain, would be over. Forever.

I'm now facing rock bottom and I know I have to get help. The depression is back full force, and I can't get out of this alone. I have to share with someone that I am not okay. Fueled by this realization, the shame multiplies exponentially. The thoughts scream in my head, *You're a complete failure! You're an embarrassment. You're a burden on your family. You're pathetic. You're so weak!*

My sweet friend Andy tried to help me at the park. He said all the right things. Most of all, he showed that he cared about me and for that, I'll be forever grateful. His compassion was a lifeline. But I was deep in the darkness, and it was hard to take in all his practical suggestions. *You don't understand, I want to end it,* I thought, but never said to him. I was too ashamed.

Shame. It was very familiar to me. I had lived with it for years. It landed in my heart and took over as my "go to" emotion after an incident that occurred when I was seven years old.

Mom asked my two brothers, Kyle, thirteen, and Todd, fifteen, to come home that afternoon. I sat on my stepdad's lap in our kitchen as my mom stood across from us, leaning her back against the kitchen counter. Since we were never all home at this time in the afternoon, I intuitively knew something devastating had happened. I felt my body tense up, as my mom began to speak. "Your dad took his life this morning."

None of us were ever the same. To this day, I don't know how my mother gathered the strength to utter that sentence.

My sweet Daddy was gone. Shame filled me. In an instant, my seven-year-old self decided that this was somehow my fault, as children often do. I had sensed how sad he was. I remember making up songs to sing to him to make him feel better. If only I could have done more. And the shame over the way he died was there in the room with us (the stigma around mental illness and suicide was extremely strong in 1980). My tense little body didn't make a move, except to look at my brothers for clues about what I should be doing. Todd slowly stood up and walked downstairs. Kyle began screaming and crying in anger. He ran out the back door, and I could hear his anguish in the back yard. It was so heart-breaking and frightening.

I didn't shed any tears. For years, I've felt added shame and guilt for not crying right away. But that day, my mission became to please others so that I could feel safe. I already felt "different" with divorced parents. The shame of losing my Daddy this way fed my shame even more. When people said they were sorry about my dad, I sensed their discomfort and would quickly say, "I'm doing okay." And smile. When I became aware that certain people blamed my mother for my father's death, I took on that guilt as my own. Years later, I learned how unfair it was for them to blame her, but by then I had spent years protecting her in my mind.

I made an agreement all those years ago. I would do my best to be "perfect" as a way to run from all the shame. I didn't know at the time that I could never run fast enough. No one can.

The more I tried to run from the shame, the stronger the shame grew. For decades, I hid my true feelings to appear "perfect," "OK," and "no trouble at all." I was a cheerleader, a national pageant girl, a winter homecoming queen. I felt like an imposter: more shame. I felt embarrassment over my need for everyone to like me (it felt like dying when someone didn't like me), which led to more shame. I never allowed myself to express anger. In fact, I felt intense shame for merely feeling anger. I was terrified of hurting someone's feelings. I couldn't bear more guilt. Though I received a scholarship to law school, I couldn't commit. I couldn't get clarity on what I wanted to do with my life because I was completely out of touch with my own feelings. More shame.

I carried that guilt and continued to suppress my feelings through my childhood and college years without seeking any help. Finally, all the shame and anger spilled out of me in the form of unstoppable tears. I couldn't function. A recent college graduate with honors, I rocked myself back in forth in my bed and wished that I could trade lives with someone else. The pain was too much.

I ultimately told my mother I needed professional help. She had a hard time accepting this. After what had happened to my dad, it terrified her to face the fact that "her baby" was having mental health issues.

My life definitely improved once I got help. I was diagnosed with clinical depression. I began taking an antidepressant and going to therapy, which helped me tremendously. The suffocating weight of deep depression began to lift, and I began to feel like me again. I could finally breathe! And eventually, I found my joy again. I gratefully discovered I could not only handle life, but was able to actually embrace and enjoy it.

It was then that I began to remember my passion for creativity and, specifically, for acting. I began working in sales and taking professional acting classes. I absolutely loved acting! I began booking local jobs and even received my Screen Actors Guild Membership. Industry professionals began telling me that this quick success was a sign that perhaps I should try my luck in a bigger market.

When reps from The Academy of Dramatic Arts came to town to hold auditions for their summer program, I signed up. I was accepted and took off for California. I remember flying from St. Louis to Los Angeles on July 4th, 1998 . . . Independence Day. How perfect for this life-long Missouri girl. It felt amazing to be pursuing my dreams.

While still studying in St. Louis, a fellow actor shared a book with me that changed my life: *The Artist's Way*, by Julia Cameron. The daily tool she prescribes, "Morning Pages," is powerful, to say the least. Three pages of longhand, stream of consciousness writing done first thing in the morning, before all of my "people-pleasing" defenses were up, was huge for me. This tool introduced me to my authentic feelings. It reminded me of the intuitive gifts I had been aware of as a child but had largely ignored in order to appear "normal." The Morning Pages deepened my connection to God, giving me the courage to expand my life and get on that plane.

The California adventure was filled with highs: performing with an improv troupe, performing in plays and receiving positive reviews, studying acting and human behavior with a brilliant coach, landing a spot in a wildly successful exercise video, P90X, and meeting the love of my life.

There were also lows . . . the depths of which I had not seen before. I was still running from the shame inside me. I was desperate to achieve "success" as an actress because I thought that would make the shame go away. It would mean I had "approval and safety." When success didn't come, the shame I felt from not making enough money to support myself consumed me and nearly did me in.

I worked for a while as a receptionist at a brokerage firm, but felt I needed more flexibility for auditions. So I became certified as a personal trainer and started my own business. I did have success with my business, but not enough to completely cover acting classes and expensive LA rent, food, and utilities. I began digging a deeper and deeper hole for myself, which led to more debilitating shame. I started to feel like I had a gambling problem. I would think, *OK, it's time to move somewhere more affordable and give up this acting thing* and then I would have some casting director tell me, "You could be on a sitcom tomorrow!" So I would stay . . . and sink deeper.

Particularly shameful was borrowing money from family and friends to cover my expenses. This felt horrible. I would talk myself into being determined to make this acting career succeed so I could pay my debts off quickly and finally feel good about myself. The pressure grew. And the thoughts I had about myself spiraled down. The voice in my head became vicious.

About one year before I hit my lowest point on that California day when I contemplated suicide on my way to meet Andy, I met the love of my life, Stephen. He was talented, funny, sweet, and gorgeous. I felt like I had stumbled upon my own Brad Pitt! The endorphins of new love lifted me for a while, but my financial situation and lack of career success eventually triggered a new level of depression in me. On top of everything else, I feared Stephen would realize what a mess I was and run for the hills.

How much of a mess was I? A few months before that day when I considered walking into oncoming traffic, I stood looking in an open kitchen cabinet in my apartment. My roommate, a close friend, had recently asked me to please stop eating her food. I was mortified that she had to ask me this. As I was looking in the cabinet, I actually thought to myself, *Would she notice if one can of dog food was gone?* I didn't eat it. But from that day on, I've completely understood why someone would.

My talk with Andy convinced me it was time to call my mom. While I don't recall the specifics of that conversation, I'm quite sure I mostly just cried into the phone. She quickly moved into action calling my brothers, Todd and Kyle. Todd and his wife, Kim, suggested I move to Austin and stay with them for a while until I could get back on my feet. Kyle and Todd loaned me money to refund my Personal Training clients who had just purchased new training packages. My roommate, Julie, graciously understood my situation and assured me she could find someone else to move in. And my sweet boyfriend, Stephen, quickly moved past his initial shock upon hearing the news that I was moving to Texas and became my biggest supporter as I took the necessary steps to get healthy again. I can never thank these people enough. They saved my life.

I got back on my feet pretty quickly in Austin. Therapy, an antidepressant, lots of time with family, and a steady income through a pharmaceutical sales job all helped immensely. Soon, I was feeling healthy again. Stephen and I got married and settled down in California. I was able to get a transfer with my pharma company.

Things were going well. I made the decision to go off my antidepressant before becoming pregnant with our first child. Our son Wyatt was born in 2008. Logan, our second son, was born in 2013. They are sweet, smart, fun, loving, amazing, and hilarious. They are our world, and I can't imagine having missed out on the chance to be their mom . . . nor can I imagine depriving the world of their bright lights.

Life was good, but not without struggles. California was still expensive, my husband is a bit of a neat freak, and my messy ways can drive him crazy. I tend to take things too personally and get my feelings hurt. Our boys are wonderful, but they can fight with each other to such a degree that they make me long for solitude. But overall, things were pretty fantastic. Until they weren't.

After twelve years of not needing medication, perimenopause and stress from a cross-country move caused my depression and anxiety to hit me like an unexpected steam roller. This time brought something new: scary derealization panic attacks. These attacks were persistent feelings of being disassociated from my body.

During the worst attack, I yelled for Stephen to come sit by me on the couch and hold me so the "something" couldn't take me away. I had never been more terrified. I knew it was time to get help again. I really struggled with the choice to start an antidepressant this last time. I prayed. I made an appointment with a therapist. I cried uncontrollably on the way to the pharmacy to pick up my prescription. In the end, I did what was right for me and my family. I'm so grateful. I got my life back. I got me back.

Though medication was a lifeline for me at different times in my life, it wasn't sufficient. Therapy and working with gifted teachers and coaches made all the difference for me. My thoughts were off. My limiting beliefs had created long-standing blind spots that were keeping me in a very small "safe" box. I was suffocating in the box but couldn't see it. I'm forever grateful that God led me to the perfect helpers on my path. My willingness to grow brought the teachers I needed.

Each time the depression came, I felt the shame of failure, even though logically, I knew it was a disease. Coming out the other side this last go-around, I decided to stop letting shame win. Shame loves it when we don't talk because that's how it stays alive. That's how it stays powerful.

To take my power back from shame, I had to begin sharing my true self with others, not the version of me I thought they wanted to see. At one time, this seemed quite impossible and dangerous to me. Thankfully, I learned certain truths that transformed my thinking and set me free from shame. I offer them here for you to take with you on your own journey.

# PATH TO YOUR POWER

## BREAK FREE FROM SHAME

Throughout my life experiences, and as I've reflected back on the toughest times, I realized that there are five truths I finally live by that make all the difference for me. I'd like to share them with you in hopes that they bring you some peace, comfort, and healing.

You don't need to be perfect to be loved. Many of us know this intellectually but have opposite thoughts under the surface. You don't need to pretend to be someone else or hide your true feelings in order to control how another person sees you. Real love and genuine connection can only be felt if you're being authentically you.

What other people think of you is none of your business. What a relief to know you can stop trying to control everyone's reaction to you. You can let others have their feelings, whatever they may be. After all, their thoughts say so much more about what they think of themselves than what they think of you. What others think of you is truly none of your business. Yay!

Your business is nobody else's business. This is such great news! For years, I felt guilty whenever something would go my way. I felt as if my success was taking away something from someone else. I would strive to be perfect, but immediately feel guilty about any success I achieved. It was a constant roller coaster of "not enough/too much." What a relief to know we don't have to justify our income, our success, our joy. We can freely focus on being the best version of ourselves and creating lives we love. This one has actually been huge for me. Is it possible that it is for you, too? Shame tells us that we're not deserving, not worthy. Shame is a liar. And your good fortune takes nothing away from anyone else. It often proves helpful to others in finding their own!

You belong to God. For me, this means: as long as God approves, I'm good (because heaven knows I will never win the approval of all the earthly beings I encounter). What a relief! When you think of all the energy we people-pleasers have spent, eliminating the striving for the approval of others is liberating! Tons of energy freed up to work on your own growth and to connect more with your creator. An entire world may open up to you by fully embracing this one. If it does, please write to me and tell me all about it. I'd love to hear your transformational stories!

Joy is your birthright. Do whatever it takes to find it. As long as you're not harming anyone else, you are allowed to do what brings you joy. This may mean increased self-care, solitude, therapy, cross-country moves, etc. This may mean setting long overdue boundaries with loved ones. This may mean putting yourself on your priority list for the first time. It's necessary. This is a powerful tool for kicking shame to the curb. Again, you are stepping into your worthiness.

## ABOUT

Holding a BA in Speech Communication and her health coach certification from the Institute for Integrative Nutrition, Audra Zimpel is an intuitive, transformational life/wellness coach who helps women find expansive joy and confidence so they can create the lives of their dreams! Her gratitude for her own journey through darkness fuels her deep passion for helping others shine, both inside and out.

She lives with her husband, Stephen, two sons, Wyatt and Logan, and an Australian Shepherd, Bindi, in Cumming, Georgia. She considers high quality chocolate a necessity in life.

Be sure to request a free copy of ***The Pink Pages***, a compilation of inspirational messages focused on leading you back to the wisdom of your heart. Asking your heart for guidance, then selecting and reading a Pink Page, can be a powerful light on your own journey out of shame and into joy. Just go to this link https://www.AudraZimpel.com/resources to claim your gift.

To learn more about Audra's private coaching and consulting, visit her website, https://www.AudraZimpel.com.

# NOTES AND REFLECTIONS

May you always speak your truth with love and light
May you always be connected to your heart
Much love and hugs
Love, Christine

# CHAPTER 11

# I LOVE YOU MORE BY CHRISTINE N. COLE

*Grief, panic attacks, and unimaginable loss lead to spiritual exploration and intuitive insight for channeling passed loved ones' messages through art.*

I arrive at the hospital with my mom and brother. The emergency room staff leads us to him. I feel like I'm in a movie, watching others play out this scene. This can't be happening. I'm not ready. He is on the table, just lying there. His head rests to the right, his eyes are open, and he has a tube emerging from his throat. His stomach moves like a wave in the ocean as the nurses perform CPR. They rotate one after the other for an hour. I feel the strangest sense of calm while my mother and brother stand behind me sobbing. I reach out and touch his right foot. I think, *You can stop now*. The rest of my family arrives. We surround him, softly reciting the Lord's Prayer through our tears. I then get close to him and whisper, "I love you more, Daddy."

It's over. He's gone. How am I supposed to live now?

My husband, John, and I moved back to my home state of Massachusetts after being away for nine years. We had just completed our fourth and final military transfer. I expected my move back home to be easy, but it wasn't. I faced many obstacles: the move, living at my parents' house in a tiny room, building our own house, and dad in the hospital for two weeks. It was overwhelming. My world spun out of control. I quickly became a shell of myself, living small and in the shadows. Then the unthinkable happened: everything turned black. I felt heaviness and sadness, emptiness, anger, and grief; it consumed every aspect of me. I didn't know why; there was no end in sight.

The feelings lingered. The week before Christmas, dad passed out at a funeral. He had gained twenty-six pounds of fluid from medication he took for a back injury. Thankfully, he was home for the holidays, but had not fully recovered before insisting on taking his vacation to Florida in January.

My dark feelings continued while they were away. Dad was back in the hospital. He checked himself out after eleven days. When I spoke to him, he didn't sound right. He talked nonsense for brief moments and coughed in between. He attributed his symptoms to being in the hospital. Later, I discovered the hospital had not quarantined those with whooping cough; he'd been exposed to the contagious disease.

The dismal energy I felt intensified when dad was rushed to the hospital for the second time. He was shaking uncontrollably and vomiting. He was admitted to the critical care unit with a 108-degree fever, whooping cough, septic infection in his left leg, and atrial fibrillation. They immediately intubated him and shocked his heart to regulate the rhythm. We were told the next twenty-four hours were the most critical.

Not knowing if he would die, five of us traveled to be with my parents. By the grace of God, my father survived and was awake when I got there. The man laying before me was not my father: the vibrant, strong man who'd taught me the importance of a life of faith, prayer, love, family, and service to others. This man was weak, frail, and broken. This scared me. I had to dig deep to find the courage and strength not to cry. My heart broke as tears rolled down his cheeks. I felt helpless.

A week later I took the long train ride from New England to Florida. I had a grim feeling that dad was at the end of his life, but I kept this to myself. I was anxious and nervous; I felt like I was losing my mind. I thought, *How do I process this? I can't lose my Daddy. How am I going to live without him? I don't know how to let him go!*

I made a conscious decision that it was not about me. I had to be strong for them. I was here to support them. Yet there were moments I felt I had reached my breaking point.

The cardiologist then told us that dad was having kidney failure and heart failure, both of which were fatal. He was not a good candidate for dialysis because of his heart. We were told to make him comfortable and let him die. We refused; the doctor told us we were selfish for making him suffer. Mom decided it was time to go home, dad and mom in a medical RV and me on the train.

For the next few months, I worked with dad nearly every day. By the summer, he was the man I remembered. His heart had even recovered to the point he could begin dialysis.

I was physically and emotionally worn out from countless hours spent at the hospital and rehabilitation at home. I lost confidence in myself. I was isolated in my emotions and neglected my husband and dog. It was one continuous drain because I never took time for self-care — there wasn't any time for me. I dreamt of leaving, releasing responsibility for everyone. But I couldn't. I felt trapped.

And then I found animal communication. AC brought me hope when I needed it most. After a brief introduction, I joined the eighteen-month program and discovered a community where I fit in and felt connected, one that I so desperately needed. I learned to communicate with animals who were living and those who had crossed the Rainbow Bridge, and how to practice Emotional Freedom Technique and scalar wave energy healing. It was the first step in finding myself again.

In October, my intuition warned me for the first time that tremendous loss was coming. My anxiety and severe panic attacks resurfaced. What I didn't realize was my intuition was also warning me that dad was going to pass away.

March arrived. I was planning my husband's retirement ceremony from military service; COVID-19 was officially declared a pandemic. This preceded a series of tragedies for my family.

Dad fell in the bathroom and hit his head on the tub at 5:00 am on Friday morning, March 27th. After a long day, we got him home from the ER. My friend and I decided to perform a scalar wave session on him. It seemed to work. However, on Sunday, he took a turn for the worse. He was in so much pain that he was sobbing, saying he wanted to die. We did a second scalar wave session that night.

I didn't like what I saw.

His lower body looked like dark, shriveled-up coal. When we reached his throat center, I saw bright red tubes of light swirling around his throat. At the top of his head, I saw him laying on a concrete slab dressed as a king. He was wearing chainmail, with a blue and silver tunic with a crest on the front, holding a sword in the center. He was surrounded by tiny white flowers. I was afraid this meant he was going to die, but when?

On Monday, March 30, 2020, dad was looking good. He was alert and himself. As he was getting ready for dialysis, in an instant, he went limp. His face was blank. My brother and I struggled to get him out of the bathroom. He stared off over my left shoulder and I knew he was seeing angels.

It took everything in me not to break down sobbing.

We got to dialysis; I sat with him telling him how strong he was as I clutched his left arm like a scared little girl. I brought him back to the dialysis machine and got him settled in the chair; the chair where he would spend the last hours of his life. I regret not taking him home and not staying longer when my intuition guided me to, but I was so caught up in my emotions that I couldn't stay.

I said, "I love you more."

He replied, "I loved you first."

These were our last words to one another, the last time I saw him alive.

Dad was rushed to the hospital. I called the emergency room and the nurse told me, "If this man were my father, I would be here." I franticly sent a text to my family to get to the hospital *now*!

He passed at 9:00 pm that evening.

Now I'm totally disconnected from my emotions. They reside outside of me. I can see them, and I am aware of them, but I can't feel them in my body. I've completely shifted to work mode. The disconnect made sharing the news and assisting with the funeral arrangements effortless, things on a to-do list.

Two days later my uncle passed away from heart failure. Then I lost my father's sister, my cousin, and my father's sister-in-law within the next five months.

I remained detached from my emotions. Between March and August, I completed the spring intensive with AC, helped my mother plan my father's funeral and celebration of life Mass, completed two week-long courses, continued going to animal communication classes, and joined another six-month program.

The Animal Communication school introduced me to Allyson Roberts that May. Allyson is a life coach who teaches Personalized Science, a combination of mindset work and spirituality. At the time, I had no idea how much of an impact she'd have on my life.

My grief finally caught up with me in August when my deeply hidden emotions came rushing forward and hit me like a freight train. I spent my days avoiding life, sitting in front of the television with lots of junk food. I was angry, sad, and lethargic. While I showed up to my classes, I abandoned the journaling and mindset work. This feeling got old, so I started walking every day by myself. I was so angry that I cried with each step. I walked past a black SUV and I thought, *If someone jumped out and attacked me right now, would I fight back?* Probably not.

Despite living in the deepest part of my grief, I was still open to receiving messages. This one came through loud and clear:

> *Our loved ones are not lost, gone, or forever removed from our lives. Our loved ones left this life so they could rise to a greater calling. Their purpose expands beyond the physical world. Their abilities are limitless and when we quiet our humanness and sit in pure love and gratitude, we can hear them and witness how bright they shine. They are opening possibilities for us that we can't even comprehend. This is bigger than us. They strengthen our connection to God and pure love if we are willing and open to all the light we truly deserve and are worthy of.*
>
> *I encourage everyone to embrace their grief, embrace the loss, and allow it to process. We and our emotions are energy; we can't dissolve it or make it go away, but we can transform it. We can create something new from it. This is our purpose to*

*create and transform. God and the universe support us if we are willing to let go of the fear, lower vibrations, and negativity to embrace our strength, courage, and love. When we do this, we remember and awaken to who we really are, our truth, ourselves. Thank you, Daddy. I love you.*

*Daddy is still here in a higher form. We are not lost. We convince ourselves we are. We are strong, but we feel lost because sometimes the fog rolls in and we can't see what is in front of us. If we trust ourselves, our inner guidance, and move forward, we will stay on the right path and when the fog lifts, we will see how bright we truly shine. We are an example to the world around us, holding space for others to recognize their light has not been dimmed.*

Allyson helped me realize I was angry because he physically left. I reconnected with him after being absent for nine years, able to hug, kiss, and spend so many precious moments with him. It was too soon for him to leave. My Daddy left me.

I came across a twenty-two-day painting and meditation class that focused on Tara, the female Buddha. I scrolled past the Facebook post several times before acknowledging the tap on my shoulder to sign up.

I was resistant; I had no idea why, but I decided to follow through. With each aspect of Tara, I would feel her energy within me helping me to release the different emotions trapped inside. This was an exploration into my true self. The pieces were falling into place, and I took a deep breath and sighed. I was now learning that it is not happening to me, but **for** me; showing me how to expand and to no longer live small.

Life began feeling more positive. Not only did I make it through the painting course, but I was also journaling again, doing my thought models, and looking forward to my next session with Allyson. As I spoke to her, I recalled the last twenty-two days. She suggested I use my animal communication and new intuitive painting skills to bring healing messages to people.

This was how Soul Paintings was born.

Allyson volunteered to be my first client. Although nervous, and not having any idea what I was doing, I sat in my chair, grounded myself, and immediately received an image. I picked up my drawing pad and translated the image to paper. I showed Allyson the final product. She was stunned. I had no idea it was her loved one reassuring her that he is always with her. It was at that moment that I realized I am a communicator, translator, and vessel for healing. This is my purpose.

What started out as a dismal and dark year ended in the light. Although I missed my dad terribly, I completed Animal Communication school, agreed to write this chapter, and started art coaching training. I continue to help people with Soul Paintings. Mindset work, journaling, and painting allowed me the space needed to process my emotions and discover who I really am. I have a tribe of like-minded beings who understand, support, and love me without judgement.

God, or the Universe, pushes you out of your comfort zone, giving you the opportunity to rediscover yourself. If you are willing and open to receiving, you will acquire a tremendous gift: yourself. Within this acquisition of truth, love, and light, the ability to raise the vibration of the world increases substantially. What a beautiful world it can become.

I will always tell my Daddy, “I love you more.” The only difference is that I now love myself, too.

# PATH TO YOUR POWER

## FINDING YOUR WAY BACK TO YOU

There is no perfect time to lose a loved one and no amount of preparation will make the grief, anger, and sadness any easier to bear. If we can allow ourselves to find the gifts within the pain and loss, it's life changing. These five building blocks are the foundation for a new life. I share them with you in hopes that you find your way through the darkness to the light. I send an abundance of love and hugs to you on your journey to finding your truth.

Honor your emotions. It is easy to dismiss our emotions and feelings, to be numb and pretend everything is okay when we are dying inside. Allow yourself to be vulnerable. Give yourself some grace. Express your emotions through any artistic modality that calls to you.

Allow transformation through your pain. Yes, it is possible to transform through pain. Pain creates space of infinite possibilities. It is within this space that our strength, courage, passion, and light are revealed. Be open and willing to receive this gift. Your willingness brings awareness to the subtle tap on your shoulder guiding you to the next step on your path.

Acknowledge the tap on your shoulder. The tap on the shoulder from the Universe can be unexpected and may not make sense. It is, after all, a clue to our next step. Things may not work out but consider this: maybe the experience itself is the lesson. Experience is valuable regardless of the form it takes. Trust the Universe and its guidance to lead you down the right path.

Trust the Universe. Trusting in the Universe is trusting a higher power, ourselves, and our intuition. God, or the Universe, pushes you out of your comfort zone, giving you the opportunity to rediscover who you are, if you are willing and open.

Seek help. It is easy to be blinded and consumed by doubt, stress, anxiety, and fear. We can feel trapped. Trusting the Universe and your intuition is challenging when you are feeling chaotic and confused. This is when you know it is time to ask for help. A coach, therapist, or someone you trust can guide you. They can help to bring clarity to your life when it seems cloudy. Through their support and love, you discover self-love and gratitude.

## ABOUT

Holding a Bachelor of Science in Communications and a Bachelor of Arts in Graphic Design from Salem State College, Christine N. (Daigle) Cole is best known for her Soul Paintings. Combining her natural intuition along with her love for painting and the arts, Christine taps into loved ones who have crossed over and brings their message to life through art. Her paintings are unique, one-of-a-kind pieces that are changing the lives of people all over the world. The cool fact about Christine's work is that she also channels messages from our beloved pets who have crossed the rainbow bridge. To schedule a session to receive your message from the Divine, contact Christine at soulpaintings72@gmail.com.

When Christine is not bringing people to tears with her miraculous work, she is managing her household where her sweet dog,

Milkbone, takes up most of her time. Christine believes that family should be a high priority, so she also devotes a lot of time to them. Christine also can be found online teaching others how to tap into their artistic abilities through the healing arts.

## NOTES AND REFLECTIONS

# NOTES AND REFLECTIONS

# CHAPTER 12

# A LITTLE BETTER . . . BY JENNIFER ETZWILER

*Years of feeling abandoned along with physical pain robbed all hope for a promising future. A sick cat, an old acquaintance, and an energy communication reveals unexpected insights to help start the healing process.*

My precious fur baby, MissKitty, that I care about more than my own life, is suddenly sick. I wake up from a dead sleep to her throwing up constantly for an hour. There is a sinking feeling of helplessness and fear deep in my body as I see her so miserable, out of control, and vomiting so hard that I can see the muscles work all down the length of her body.

I manage to get her into the car. We make it to the vet, only to be given some anti-nausea medicine and sent home. I have no diagnosis and no instructions for what to do if this happens again. I feel even more helpless and scared. I have no idea what happened to cause this.

In the eighteen years of her life, MissKitty has been my constant companion; she is seldomly more than a few feet from me. She is the one friend and support buddy that is a constant through my years of chronic pain, illness, and depression. I'm home with her all the time because I have not held a job for her entire life span. When I say that I love her more than I love myself, I really mean that. *She* hasn't left me like the others have.

I won't accept the lack of a firm diagnosis and treatment plan, so I set out to look for a solution and an end to the uncertainty. As I rack my brain for some appropriate action, I remember someone I knew years before.

Beverly is an animal communicator I met when I was in my mid-twenties. I was immediately fascinated with her talent. You can *talk* to *animals*? You can do it *for a living*? Where do I sign up?!

We had lost touch over the years, but I knew that if anyone could help me figure out what was wrong with my companion, it was her. It was a relief to realize there might be someone able to talk to MissKitty to find out what she's feeling and what symptoms were bothering her.

I look up Beverly and discover she still lives nearby. So, I call her.

**Finding Beverly and learning from her wisdom inspired an idea that forever changed the course of my life.**

It's hard for me to remember a time when I didn't struggle with depression in its many forms. I've hit rock bottom more than once.

At one time, I enjoyed my job at the call center of a major retailer. I enjoyed interacting with people. I loved the challenge of problem-solving. Then I was involved in three car accidents in the short span of five months' time. My car was totaled in the last one. Injuries ended my career and left me in severe pain.

I've tried so many things to make my depression bearable, I have lost count. I have worn myself out chasing all the things that I believed would help by providing a quick fix, seeking the magic bullet to change my life. I have bought self-help books about religion, spirituality, tarot, crystals, Wicca, and other topics by the armful. I took heavy-duty pain killers, drowned out the reality of my life with television fantasies, and wallowed in negative thoughts constantly. I still felt awful.

I'm an introvert; socializing can be difficult. I have made excuses to the few friends I have so I don't have to go out and socialize. No one invites me anywhere anymore. When I was meeting up with friends, it was embarrassing to have nothing to talk about because I wasn't doing anything. Admittedly, it takes so much energy just to shower that I need a long nap afterward. Who wants to hear about that? I certainly don't want to share all of it. To this day, the stress of trying to make sure I feel well enough to go out can make me physically ill.

Maybe this struggle started when my grandfather died. It felt like I was all alone at eighteen months old. I don't mean physically alone. I don't know how I know it, but a bond existed between us that was special. It was filled with mutual love and trust that I have been trying to replace ever since.

I was so young that I have few real memories. I've filled in the missing pieces from pictures and home movies. It doesn't matter. I know how I feel. The more issues that I heal, the more the deep wounds keep revealing themselves. No matter how much I try to replace the feeling of connection, it still seems impossible. In every one of my close relationships, something is missing.

I try to give deep, unconditional love to other people in hopes that I will get it in return. It never works. Expecting others to behave the way I would is a recipe for disappointment. Each person lives a different experience that leads to their reactions; no one has lived the exact same life as me, so I cannot expect them to have the same responses. People are not mind readers either. How can they possibly know what I need if I don't tell them?

There was a time when I believed that everyone that I cared about left me. Everywhere I looked, I had proof. My grandfather died when I was a toddler. I'm not married and have been single for more than ten years. My partner left me to find his happiness at a time I could barely get off the couch due to extreme anxiety. I lost both my father and my stepfather in just over a three-year period. With this all happening around me, I couldn't see past it.

My thoughts continued to spiral downward. I was replaying old stories. I tried to keep the peace between my divorced parents. I wasn't good enough unless I was the smartest. I needed to be better than everyone else just to be noticed. I still sometimes believe that if I am not the best, no one will love me. Trying and failing was worse than not trying at all. I replayed every regret in my life. With all that spinning around all the time, I was angry; being angry all the time was my normal.

People offered unsolicited advice or told me what to do, which led to me feeling defensive and judged. I felt the need to explain why the advice wasn't working. It was maddening and left me asking myself the questions, "Don't you think I thought of that?" and, "If it were all that simple, don't you think I would have done it already?"

On the other hand, I thought that I needed someone to tell me what to do because I didn't think I knew how to be an adult. I struggled to pay my bills on time or on budget. I didn't have enough money. I wasn't eating well. Making decisions for everything else was too overwhelming. I was supposed to be enjoying adulthood, but I felt like I was sinking.

It was difficult to get out of bed. My health was slowly declining, which made my body feel like it was aging at an accelerated rate. I felt so much older. As you can imagine, that just added to the depression. Watching my stepfather go from active and independent to bedridden fed into my idea that that could be me one day.

My mind slipped into its familiar story. I am an only child. My mother is an only child, and when she's gone, I will be *Alone*, with a capital 'A.' The struggle was real and one I still combat to this day.

One of my escapes was television. It was tricky, though, because there were times when the fear showed up out of nowhere. I could be engrossed in a show that I loved and then, without any warning at all, I would find myself in tears. Sometimes it happened if it was too quiet while I was trying to fall asleep. With nothing to distract me from my thoughts in the dark, the tears streamed down my face, into my hair, and onto my pillow. I experienced heaving sobs that turned into painful headaches. I finally succumbed to sleeping with the television on as a way to cope. Sleep was my escape from all the fears and pain.

**Just when I thought everything was lost, I reconnected with Beverly.**

Even though I originally called Beverly because my cat was sick, we barely talked about MissKitty during what became weekly appointments. I thought I was calling an animal communicator, but what I got was so much more.

Beverly explained that her style of communication is all energy. She talks to guides and crossed-over loved ones, too, calling them "your people." We talked about whatever was going on that was bothering me. As I poured out my heart, I cried until I had a headache, but

I kept going back. I was finally accepting the help I needed from a person I trusted.

I couldn't help but think that even *my cat* knew I needed help. There is no doubt that the sessions took a physical toll on my body, but emotionally, I felt freer and more expansive. It was an added benefit that MissKitty was better because I was better.

As my relationship with Beverly progressed, I learned that our companion animals are more sensitive to energy and emotions. Unfortunately, MissKitty was taking on my sadness and depression energetically as a way to try to heal me. Neither Beverly nor I were too surprised by it, but what took us aback was that MissKitty wasn't processing or releasing the energy. Instead, she held onto it, and that was what made her sick. I was in such a dark place, but this all made sense.

Beverly rarely told me what I wanted to hear. She told me what I *needed* to hear. She repeated the same things as many times as necessary until I understood them completely. She had the patience of a saint. It changed me.

My biggest turning point during our work together came during a conversation about feeling "better."

"Does that feel better?" she asked.

In my gut, I knew it was important for me to qualify my answer, "A little. It's not *ALL* better, but it's a little better."

Beverly's response was a major pivot point in my life. Her words were like music to my soul. "A little better *is* better, Jennifer. A little better is all it needs to *be* better," she said.

I sat with that for several breaths. My mind was blown. I'd been muddling through life looking for "all better" and felt anything less wasn't good enough. I was either "all better" or I was still sick. I was so focused on the negative that I wasn't appreciating *any* of the little wins.

Over time, as Beverly and I worked together, I took small steps and my life began to transform into one with meaning and a feeling of usefulness. I've developed a skill to focus on the positive. I still occasionally allow myself to wallow in the mucky emotions. I'm a work in progress. I'm okay with that.

It took me a while to get to this point and to create a life that is as close to normal as possible during a pandemic. These days, I leave the house every couple of days. I do the grocery shopping myself and skip the delivery.

I found a spiritual community where I feel safe and accepted, and I serve as a volunteer there.

I take classes to continue my personal development.

I joined an amazingly supportive group coaching program.

My relationship with my mom is closer and more meaningful.

I have made friends. I like them, and I believe that they like me for who I truly am.

I have responsibilities. They are not too scary, and I fulfill them regularly. I commit to being there and having people depend on me.

The best part is that I show up for *myself*. When I don't feel like it, I push myself to do it anyway. I do it because I feel better afterward. Even if I don't feel better while doing the task, I feel better because I showed up for me.

Don't get me wrong, my life is not perfect. There really is no magic bullet or quick fix. Each day brings new opportunities to stretch my adulting skills, to become the person I need to be and have always wanted to be, to learn to communicate better, and to move outside my comfort zone.

Healing is messy and uncomfortable. It can be terrifying to face the things you've been avoiding for years. None of the things I've had to face were nearly as scary as I thought they were going to be, and I felt a lot better in the long run.

In this life, very little is about all or nothing. I get it. When you are in pain, you want it to stop — right now. Remember that it took your whole life to get to where you are; things are not going to be perfect overnight. You would not start jogging for the first time at forty and expect to be able to win a marathon after a week of practice.

Give whatever you do a fair chance to see improvement. Any little bit of better is still better than it was before.

## NOTES AND REFLECTIONS

## PATH TO YOUR POWER

### BREATHE (AND OTHER SIMPLE THINGS THAT WILL SAVE YOU)

After years of therapy, and searching for the BIG answer, I found that the things that calm me the most are the simple things. They are the things readily and easily available to us, but we think they either won't work or, in my case, "It can't be that simple." It is. Here's to your easier path out of pain.

Breathe. Just breathe. Pick one part of your body to focus on and feel how it's affected by every breath. I like to pick a spot on the end of my nose, or in my chest, to focus on. How does it feel as I breathe in and out? If my mind wanders, I bring it back to focus on breathing. Focusing on breathing helps quiet those spinning thoughts that can pull me down the rabbit hole.

Reach out for the help you need. I know you've read this a few times already. Here's the thing. We mean it! If you are struggling, what's going to happen is that you're going to try doing the same things you've always done. It will feel better for a few days or months, if you're lucky, maybe even years. But if you keep ending up right back here, please ask for help.

Set up a daily check-in. As I look back over my journey of the past five years, I see where I just let days pass me by. Now, I have a daily check-in, which I highly recommend. Take the time to sit with your feelings and thoughts. Journal, if it's safe to do so, and write out everything you're experiencing in that moment. Just getting it out helps relieve the pressure of holding it all in.Find a distraction. Sometimes it helps to have a temporary distraction. I call this a mini self-vacation. Set a timer and walk away from everything you're doing or that's going on around you. Even if it means going to the bathroom for ten minutes and allowing the water from the sink to run over your hands. Get away to get grounded.

Focus on something that you feel better about. There's always ice cream (or your favorite food), the way your pet's fur feels against your hand when you pet them, smelling the flowers in the garden with grandma . . . anything that you feel better about. You'd be amazed at how finding the thing that brings a smile to your face for a moment can change the course of your entire day.

## ABOUT

Jennifer has an amazing time dancing off-beat to life's music. She found non-traditional methods that work for her to live with depression. She is an intuitive and talks to animals, arachnids, and sometimes even people. If you are curious about what your animal friend might be thinking or saying to the next-door neighbor's cat, then you can contact her at jennifer.etzwiler@gmail.com.

When Jennifer isn't filling the shoes of Dr. Doolittle, she can be found enjoying creating with hobbies that include knitting and jewelry making. She is also frequently found on Zoom, connecting with others and learning new things — something which is also her passion.

## CHAPTER 13

# FINDING THE MAGIC WITHIN BY CARRI BETTS

*A life of abuse, abandonment, and emotional pain created physical illness that caged an otherwise active lifestyle. Connecting with nature and learning to listen to her intuition opened the door for personal healing as well as a successful career as a Healer.*

"Let me in! We need help!" I scream as I pound furiously on my nana's door in the middle of the night.

Panicked, my great-grandmother opens the door, picks me up and asks, "What's wrong?" I can barely get words out, as I am out of breath and frozen with fear, thinking my father is going to kill my mother and brother. I finally get the words out, "Call Mem and Pep!" (my father's parents). I don't have to tell her what is going on; she knows how my father gets when he is drunk.

Sitting at her kitchen table in my soiled underwear, I try to catch my breath while she makes some calls for help. I can't stop shaking and sobbing as the visions of my father and brother rolling through the hallway, beating on each other, race through my six-year-old mind. When she is finished making the calls, she wraps me in a blanket and puts me to bed, where I lay there thinking, *Am I even going to have a family to go home to in the morning?*

Early morning arrives and my mom calls to say I can come home. As I walk there, a huge pit forms in my stomach and I feel like I am going to vomit, not knowing what I was going home to. My little mind was racing. *Was my brother okay? What was our life now even going to look like? What would the teacher think of me missing school? Would everyone be ashamed of me? What would I tell my friends?* The questions were endless.

For the next few years, life always felt unsafe, never knowing when my father would have one of his rages. I lived in a never-ending state of fear. My stomach was constantly in knots which landed me in the hospital numerous times.

To escape the chaos and find peace, I created my own world outside with my "imaginary" friends and our animals, a magical world where I felt safe. I had the fairies, gnomes, wildlife, and my dogs. If I had to be inside, I isolated myself in my bedroom.

It wasn't until my mom met a man named Tony that she would find the courage to divorce my father. As a nine-year-old girl, I was devastated my parents wouldn't be together and felt a deep sense of abandonment. Our family was so imperfect, but it was my family.

Tony moved in with us. He was a funny, kind man. Although he could see I needed a father figure desperately, I pushed him away due to my own insecurities and feelings of being deserted again.

At the age of fifteen I was slinking around with a twenty-one-year-old man. I found myself sneaking out for the next three years, having sex and drinking, until my mom caught us for the final time. Feeling deeply hurt that I was repeating her same pattern with abusive men, she was so furious that she told me to pack my things and get out. It wasn't long after I moved in with him I discovered I was living with an emotionally and sexually abusive alcoholic. By the time I turned twenty-two, I couldn't take the abuse anymore, but I was still having a hard time deciding to leave. I was so afraid to be alone.

We had a weekend getaway planned and almost canceled because I had moved out a week prior. The weekend proved to be fun until we were almost home. He pulled over to find a hotel, but I was infuriated because the last thing I wanted was to spend another night with him. After hours of dealing with his manic behavior and sexual abuse, I stood in the shower feeling nauseated, worthless, and lost.

Returning home safely the next day, and desperate *now* to not *be alone*, I sought out a new guy who'd caught my attention. He was a badass biker, tall, handsome, and funny; a real charmer you could say. He totally swept me off my feet. It wouldn't be long before we moved in together. We were both working full time, which didn't allow us the freedom we wanted. When I ran into an old friend, she shared how much money she was making as a stripper. Feeling worthless anyway, I decided to give it a try, as it would allow us to do as we pleased with good money coming in.

The club I worked in permitted men to touch me. I didn't want to allow this, but I had to in order to make the money. I spent the next year high on cocaine to numb out all the pain from having to consent to their requirement. Being molested by men for money took a tremendous toll on me, making me feel even more worthless and empty, so I finally decided to hang up my stilettos and get a real job.

Although I quit stripping, we would still find ourselves wrapped up in the drug scene. Being at all the parties was a top priority, spending all of our money on drugs. Some weeks we didn't even have money for food, but then again, who wants to eat when they're high anyway?

It wasn't until after my twenty-sixth birthday celebration, on our drive home, that I realized there had to be more to life. Just living for the "good" times was getting old. I felt a deep emptiness and had no real purpose. I was so tired of not having anything, including money. Finally I was ready to change! I discovered that what I really wanted was a real home with a family I could call my own.

A month passed, and I discovered I was pregnant. It was like someone punched me in the gut. What was I going to do? Did I even want to bring a child into this world? I didn't even love myself enough to take care of me. We had nothing. How in the hell could we manage a child?

After a lot of reflection, I made the decision to have the baby. I quit doing drugs and started to find some faith in God; that is what would keep me sober throughout my pregnancy. When my daughter was born, she was, of course, pure love, joy, and light. It felt so good to have something of my very own, someone to share in my love in a very real way. My heart was so full to finally have the family I had been longing for my whole life.

While I had become a different person now with a daughter who brought me such joy, I lived in constant fear that my husband would abandon us. Even as I desperately tried to hold onto him, he told me he never wanted to be married or have a child. He was always out running with the biker pack, leaving me and my daughter for the weekend with no way to get in touch. He lied and cheated all the time.

A part of me longed for the old life, the life of parties and getting into trouble. Why do I have to always be the responsible one? Tired of being left behind and unsupported as a wife and a mom, I decided to get a sitter for the night and head out to a party. That's all it took, one party, and I started to do cocaine and drink again on the weekends.

Desperate to keep up with my husband, I left my daughter with my mom, where I knew she would be safe while we partied.

I was running a construction business with my husband, caring for my daughter, and exhausted from trying to hold onto him. The business started to fail due to the amount of drug abuse, lies, and lack of knowledge about how to be a business owner. We started struggling financially and faced eviction. We were caught up in the same cycle, only this time with a three-year-old. How were we going to get out of this one?

*Finally*, I hit the proverbial wall. I couldn't take it anymore. Although I was terrified of what lay ahead, I knew if I stayed, life would get even worse. Putting my daughter in the car, I drove to my mom's house for help. A few days later, I went back home and I asked for a divorce.

Out of desperation, we went back to my mother's house, except this time, we moved in. Living with my mother and Tony allowed me the chance to get back on my feet. I felt so embarrassed having to move back home as a thirty-year-old woman. I was also deeply ashamed of the choices I'd made in my life. I was wounded by my ex-husband's actions. I felt lost, betrayed, angry, and downright broken-hearted.

Driving around one day, lost in my thoughts, I received an intuitive message to turn down a side street in town that I'd never gone down. I looked up to see a spiritual shop called Back Door to the Moon. Walking in felt comforting as I was greeted by Moonie, a little dachshund. There was a tall woman with short black hair and red glasses named Sandi standing behind the counter.

This would become my place to escape, where I found myself getting lost in all the books, crystals, and Sandi's knowledge. She took me under her wing, teaching me all she could. I slowly began learning about energy work, spell work, tapping into my intuition, what nature has to say to us, and starting to discover who I am. For the first time in my life, I was feeling alive. I had a new job; I enrolled in massage school. Most important, my daughter and I were finally in our own place.

Just as everything was going my way, I fell ill with terrible stomach issues that led to many hospitalizations. The joint pain, swelling, and muscle pain caused me to lose my career as a massage therapist, as it worsened to the point where I couldn't even get out of bed.

Being sent from doctor to doctor, with none of them pinpointing what was wrong while writing prescriptions to mask the symptoms, left me feeling hopeless and scared. Finally, a doctor asked, "Have you been sexually abused?" My instant response was "No." This question stayed at the forefront of my mind. The question was actually my wake-up call, like this wave of wisdom came flooding in from all the knowledge I soaked up in massage school and from Sandi. I knew from all the work I did in the past how the body holds onto emotions. Now it was time to put that wisdom to use.

The first thing I did was make a decision to get better. I knew the power of the mind and that it can heal the body, so I started there. Then I thought, *What if I get a dog?* I would want a female and I would name her Stella. For a couple weeks, I thought about this often, but I was out of work, going to the food bank to feed my daughter, and could barely walk. *But what if that dog could help you walk?* I heard from out of nowhere.

About a month later I had another doctor's appointment that left me feeling even more hopeless. Even though the bloodwork didn't show anything, he gave me another prescription and wanted to send me to yet another doctor. Why couldn't anyone help me?

On the drive home I was guided to an animal shelter. Dogs have always brought me comfort, so I thought looking at the dogs would make me feel better. Sure enough, there she was! She was a black beauty with almond-shaped amber eyes and a head-tilt to die for. It was love at first sight!

I asked the attendant for her name. "Stella," she replied. I knew as soon as I heard her name, the universe had aligned our meeting. Soon after our meeting, we welcomed Stella into our family. Almost immediately I began feeling better. Stella was magical and I was the benefactor.

She helped me get out of bed in the morning and tune into my body. If I was pushing myself too hard, she would stop me in my tracks and she ALWAYS knew when I was about to have a bad flare. Through this process with her, I was able to tune into the emotions I felt. I really started evaluating my life and asked myself one question, "Was I sexually abused?"

This was not an easy question to address. When I sat with it, I realized I could feel it in my stomach. Then I started asking more questions like, "What are you holding onto?" "What are you stuffing down and not ready to face?" It was when I started asking myself those questions and really digging deep for the answers, I found some relief. I knew I had to build my immune system, eat better, and get off the medication to get better and heal.

In 2013, my abandonment issues were triggered again when I lost my stepdad, Tony, to suicide. I had no idea what to do with the pain I was feeling. In fact, it caused me to put up walls and push away loved ones. I took all that grief, anger, guilt, shame, and despair I was feeling and started planting flowers. There was something so healing about having my hands in the dirt. I began to look at other areas of my life that were broken and needed to be healed.

Spending hours getting lost in the sounds of nature, along with watching my flowers bloom, helped me to find the connection I innately had that'd been lost many years ago. I started to feel the fairies surrounding me and soon enough, I would hear my flowers telling me how they have been helping me, that I should be diving deeper into studying their healing properties. After years of working with the flowers and tapping back into my intuition, I am able to help others heal through nature, art, and following their intuition.

## NOTES AND REFLECTIONS

# PATH TO YOUR POWER

## CONNECTING WITH NATURE TO HEAL

When I began connecting with nature, almost overnight the path to begin healing from abuse, abandonment, and other emotional wounds gently revealed itself to me. It was through this connection that I reconnected with my sanity. I want this for you, also. Our world is full of magic. The more we connect with nature, the more magic that happens within us. Here are some steps to take to connect with it.

Plant some flowers. Building a relationship with them will show you how something that spends so much time in the darkness can bloom into something beautiful. You don't have to have a yard to accomplish this. Simply buy indoor plants, starting small, and witness what starts to happen in your life.

Listen to the birds. What is their song saying to you? Again, if you live in a noisy area or a place where you don't have easy access to the outdoors, all you have to do is search YouTube or Google for songbirds, choose the ones you love, and listen while you work, do chores, or as you're falling asleep.

Find a tree to sit with. Take in its strength and flexibility. I have trees in my yard, but I also love going to parks and finding a strong tree to lean against and journal. Spread a blanket, sit down, and stay awhile.

Stand with your feet firmly on the ground. This is best done with bare feet. Find a place in the grass, feel your body sink into the ground through your feet. When you're ready, close your eyes, take some deep breaths, and just feel all the abundance from the universe flowing through you. It's also a great way to release anxiety into the earth.

Leave your phone behind and take a nice long walk. Take this walk with the intention of slowing down and taking in the sights of nature. Make a mental note of any animals that cross your path. What flowers catch your eye? If you believe, each one holds a message for you.

## ABOUT

Carri Betts is an intuitive healer who uses her profound wisdom to select the most effective healing path for both people and animals. Holding certifications in Emotional Freedom Technique, Reiki, and Flower Therapy, she guides clients every step of the way with compassion, kindness, and grace. As a resin artist, Carri uses her intuition to custom design pyramids layered with the healing properties of nature to purify, cleanse, and provide continuous healing in your space. She is also profoundly gifted intuitively using all of her gifts and talents to light the path for everyone she serves. To learn more about Carri and her services, visit https://CarriBetts.com/. As a sidenote, Carri is also the Spiritual Sage for Allyson Roberts' coaching programs, running the small groups and offering additional spiritual support.

When Carri isn't changing the world, she talks to fairies, plants, and tends to her flowers, loves all over Wylie, her dog, and pours her heart into her family and friends.

# A MESSAGE FROM ALLYSON

*You didn't go through your painful stuff for nothing. It can be a new beginning.*

It's Sunday, September 11, 2016. I'm sitting in the lobby of a hotel that is connected to the Vancouver International airport looking out at the most incredible view. Even though I've just had one of the most amazing weeks of my life, something is missing. As the sun sets behind the mountains, and it's a glorious site, I feel empty. Something has to change.

As the lump forms in my throat, I take out a pen to use the thought model I learned in college: C-T-F-A-R.

The C line is our outside circumstance — our trigger. It's the thing we believe is controlling our lives. The T line is our thoughts about the circumstance. The F line is our feelings created by the thought. (Yes, feelings follow our thoughts, not the other way around, as many believe.) The A line is the action we take as a result of thoughts and feelings. The R line is the result we experience as a result of the cognitive process happening in our brain and in our actions.

The tears fall.

Circumstance-My business
Thought-I'm ignoring the calling on my heart
Feeling-Guilty
Action-Keep doing the same thing
Result-Something is missing

I stare at the napkin for TWO hours! Two long, excruciating hours. It's not like me to just freeze. After all, I'm an Aries. We get into action. But I also know that action that isn't inspired is a recipe for disaster. I think I am mostly paralyzed by the fear of reinventing myself . . . again.

It's time to make my way home. So, I collect my things, make my way through security, and board the first of three planes home.

I love to fly, but this trip is definitely different. I stare out the window. I am numb. Lost. Confused. Tired. Angry. And, yet it is SO simple. Just change my mind. I know this! I teach it. I sighed deeply and reclined my seat. I still didn't feel any peace. This wasn't like me.

The plane has to make an unexpected stop in Toronto instead of our scheduled layover in New York. It's a long and emotional story that I will take the liberty of sparing you from, but suffice it to say, I hated the fact we were landing in Toronto. My mood wasn't up for that energy. The airport holds too many memories of a love lost long ago. "Great," I hear myself say out loud to no one in particular. The Universe is definitely trying to get my attention.

After a rather lengthy deplaning process, I make my way to the Sky Club for my four-hour layover. I literally fall into my chair, take out the crumpled napkin, and stare again at my words for my C-T-F-A-R.

Here's what I know. We can be reactive and live the same patterns over and over to ad nauseum. Or we can examine what's happening in our cognitive process, take full responsibility for our life experience and change our outcome. This is where I am, in the middle. I'd been willing to write it out on a napkin a few hours earlier, think about it on the first flight, and now here I am.

Holding the napkin, actually gripping it with white knuckles, the T line jumped off the page and yelled at me!

T-I'm ignoring the calling on my heart!

"Jesus Christ!" It's a prayer and anger all in one. I think I even said it out loud because a man next to me seemed to chuckle. The thing is, I'm not laughing.

I stand and walk to the bathroom. I feel hot tears streaming down my face. Arriving in the bathroom, I check all the stalls to be sure I am alone. I look in the mirror at my tired reflection staring back at me. I watch myself say, "I don't want to reinvent myself. Again. I don't want to fail. I'm scared. Terrified, actually." I close my eyes and take a deep breath. I am sobbing now, "What if only one person shows up? What if it doesn't work? What if I'm broke . . . homeless (again)?"

I hear my mother's voice, "Look at you! You're so pathetic." She is mocking my words, "I don't wanna be homeless. What if they don't show up?"

My jaw clenches. My whole body tenses. The anger is rising up. I open my eyes and remind myself that my mother lost her power over me long ago. I remind myself of the day I took it all back from her. I remind myself that I'm here for a reason.

I pray right there in a Delta sky lounge bathroom, "God, please! Please!"

Then, the familiar voice of calm and serenity, "I won't bring you to it without seeing you through it." It is SO loud, so reassuring, so calming. There is no mistaking it.

I wash my face, straighten my clothes, and make my way back to my seat. The man who'd been amused by my despair catches my eye. His face softens and when I am settled back in my seat, he leans in my direction and says, "You're gonna be alright." I take that as a sign.

Opening my laptop case, I took out fresh paper and a different pen. Taking the deepest breath I'd taken in weeks, I wrote:

Circumstance-group coaching
Thought-It's my calling.
Feeling-Shy but willing.
Action-Put the program together.
Result-A successful program where lives are changed, dreams are realized, and goals are accomplished.

Tears fell but they were different this time. I could feel the energy coursing through my veins. I knew it was the truth. If I'm honest, I don't always love the truth in situations like this. While it's freeing, it's also life changing! Those changes are not always easy, but the rewards along the way are unexplainable. I was ready.

As I predicted, everything changed rapidly. This is what happens when we follow our true calling. The results didn't happen overnight, but ***I*** changed quickly. I worked on becoming a group leader who had thirty or more people in her six-month program. I worked on becoming a book collaborator affording the opportunity for women to have their voices heard, their businesses spotlighted, and their lives changed. I worked on becoming a Mindset Coach Certification school. I worked on becoming a Host of live events. The Universe was screaming, "There is no limit," and I yelled back, "I accept!"

Here's my message to you. Please allow this to soak in. You are powerful! Yes, you. There is a calling on your life–several of them, actually. Your life has many purposes. You were born to be here right now. You may be thinking to yourself that callings and purposes are for other people. That's simply not true. You may be thinking that it's too late, too early, too hard, too much, too…too…too. Or, if you're like me, you're thinking that there's not enough time, money, people. skills, reasons, helpers . . . . I get it! I see you!

The real deal, though, is that you're reading this. It's not a coincidence. So, here's what I'd like you to do. Join me! You're not alone. Go to your phone or iPad or computer, hell, you may be reading this on a device now, and type in www.AllysonRoberts.com. This will allow you to:

1. Join Painless Pivots to Power (a free webinar that takes place several times a year).
2. Join my Facebook community for daily support at Outrageous Results.

I also highly recommend that you re-read this book. Take a highlighter and pen and make notes all over it. Restart your healing by making a commitment to start again. Just start. Don't think about the finish line.

Thank you, my love, for being on this journey with me and the thirteen beautiful, honest, and talented women who shared their hearts and bared their souls to you. Maybe you have a story you want to share with the world, too. Maybe you know that you didn't go through your painful stuff for nothing. If you're feeling deeply inspired and want to share your story with the world, this is a very good place to start. Let's talk.

# MY PROMISE TO MYSELF

# ACKNOWLEDGMENTS

I would like to acknowledge Freda Cornelius, a client and earth angel, who set me on the path to becoming my best self by introducing me to incredible women who would become my coaches and mentors — who also deserve acknowledging. They are Lisa Nichols, Keri Murphy, and Megan Huber. Without your honesty, guidance, "sock-it-to-me" realness, and so much more, I wouldn't be the version of Allyson that I am today. So, with all of my heart, thank you!

# NOTES AND REFLECTIONS

# ABOUT THE AUTHOR

Allyson Roberts is a Cognitive Behavioral Expert with a global reach and over twenty-five years of experience. She was named to the Top 100 Coaches in the World in 2020 by Feedspot and has been featured on major networks, radio broadcasts, newspapers, podcasts, and live and virtual stages. She is the author of ***The Magic in You*** and ***Woman of Worth - Women in Business in a Changing World*** along with dozens of guest blogs.

Allyson is the creator of Personalized Science — a system that combines Science and Spirituality that promotes healthy and lasting lifestyle changes along with a renewed sense of the higher-self-connection. The Personalized Science system is being offered all over the world through Allyson's live and virtual workshops. Her mission is to show others how the brain keeps us prisoners to the past, and more importantly, teach the tools to break out of unhealthy life patterns and cycles. She wants to show people how they are the power source for their own life, and with the help of their spiritual team, can become the most powerful version of themselves. Find out more at www.AllysonRoberts.com.

Allyson lives with her adult daughter and grandson in a gorgeous city just outside of Atlanta, Georgia. She can be frequently found on the tennis court or the playground. She loves to nurture both her grandson and her inner child.

If you'd like more information about Allyson's work, visit her website (www.AllysonRoberts.com) or feel free to connect with her on social media:

Outrageous Results – Facebook Group
Outrageous Freedom – Instagram
Allyson Roberts – LinkedIn

# A SPECIAL GIFT FROM ALLYSON

Now that you've read this amazing book, you more clearly understand that you are not alone, no matter what you are facing right now. Through the moving stories inside these pages, you've discovered that there is hope, and that it's possible to accomplish the goals to make your dreams come true.

But let's face it, life can be challenging. This is especially true when you don't understand what's happening inside (or outside) of you. You do all the right things. You are "a good person." You're responsible, caring, loving, compassionate, generous, kind . . . and yet, you somehow always end up right back where you started — no matter what you try to change to create a different reality.

It's not you . . . it's your brain. It's the truth.

Your brain has a part of it called "the reptilian" and its job is to keep you safe, to keep you the same. Yet to make changes in your life and get different results than what you've had so far, you have to do things differently.

That doesn't mean go out and try many different things (or the same thing) over and over because that only yields more frustration, and you won't be any further ahead. In fact you'll likely move backwards.

To help you begin creating the right foundation for making the changes you want to make, I have prepared a special gift just for you: *Becoming the Boss of Your Brain!* This gift will help you slow down, acknowledge your feelings and emotions, and honor who you are. You've made it through all of life's challenges you've faced so far, and you **can** create a different life than the one you have right now.

Just go to AllysonRoberts.com/gift and tell us where to send it.

Thanks for letting all of us be part of your journey!

**Allyson**

Made in USA - Kendallville, IN
32489_9781737551102
12 15 2021 1746